5-Minute
BIBLE
STUDY
for
Women

Mornings in God's Word

ISBN 978-1-64352-556-3

Published by Barbour Books, an imprint of Barbour Publishing, Inc., 1810 Barbour Drive, Uhrichsville, Ohio 44683, www.barbourbooks.com

Our mission is to inspire the world with the life-changing message of the Bible.

Member of the
Evangelical Christian
Publishers Association

The
5-Minute
BIBLE
STUDY
for
Women

Mornings in God's Word

ANNIE TIPTON

BARBOUR BOOKS
An Imprint of Barbour Publishing, Inc.

Introduction

～

Every morning you wake up, you have a choice to make. What tone will you set for today? If you're not the rare soul who cheerfully bounds out of bed while whistling an early-day tune, maybe dragging yourself out of bed is the first item on your to-do list. Get ready for work? Get kids ready for the day? Coffee (and more coffee)? Breakfast? (Who has time for *that*?)

Harried mornings aren't reserved for moms or women who work outside the home. The truth is that *most* of us are rushing through our mornings, just trying to make it to the next part of the day clean, dressed, and perhaps on time. But that frenzied process often leaves us stressed. And irritable. And impatient. Not a good way to start the day!

God has so much more in store for your days, friend!

This book is intended to help you begin your day in the very best place—at the throne of God, studying His Word. It will hopefully provide an opportunity for you to open the Bible regularly and dig into a passage—even if you have only five minutes!

Minutes 1–2: **Read.** Carefully read the scripture passage for each day's Bible study.

Minute 3: **Understand.** Ponder a couple of prompts designed to help you apply the verses from the Bible to your own life. Consider these throughout your day as well.

Minute 4: **Apply.** Read a brief devotional thought based on the day's scripture. Think about what you are learning and how to apply the scriptural truths to your own life.

Minute 5: **Pray.** A prayer starter will help you to begin a time of conversation with God. Remember to allow time for Him to speak into your life as well.

May *The 5-Minute Bible Study for Women: Mornings in God's Word* help you establish the discipline of studying God's Word. Pour yourself a cup of coffee and make that first five minutes of your day count! You will find that even five minutes focused on scripture and prayer has the power to make a huge difference. Soon you will want to provide for even more time in God's Word!

Choose Extraordinary

Read Romans 12

Key Verse

Do not conform to the pattern of this world, but be transformed by the renewing of your mind.
Romans 12:2 niv

Understand

- What is one thing or who is one person you would describe as "extraordinary"? What makes this thing or person extraordinary?
- God created you for an extraordinary purpose. Think of one passion He has put in your heart. How can He use that today for great things?

Apply

Wake up; be awesome. Oh, if only it were that easy! But the messages the world shouts keep us feeling inadequate. We're not good enough, beautiful enough, smart enough, thin enough, or rich enough. Soon these messages take root in our hearts, and we're telling ourselves these same lies. Satan knows the ins and outs of that game.

But those lies don't have to be the words you focus on today. This morning, choose to make this day extraordinary by living out God's plan for your life. Romans 12 gives guidance on how to do just that. Refuse to listen to the world's lies, and instead focus on the renewal that God promises. Focus on the talents God has given you, and use them today—for His glory. Intentionally show God's love to those around you today.

Your loving heavenly Father created you for more than a mediocre existence. Choose this day and every day to live an extraordinary life in Christ.

PRAY

Father, I admit most days I feel more ordinary than extraordinary. But You call me to greatness, not because of what I can achieve but because of Your holiness and Your unending love for me. Each day I aspire to be more like You: more extraordinary than the day before. Amen.

God Knows Your Future

~

Read Jeremiah 29:1–23

KEY VERSE

"For I know the plans I have for you," says the LORD. "They are plans for good and not for disaster, to give you a future and a hope."
JEREMIAH 29:11 NLT

UNDERSTAND

- When in the past did God work in a way that you did not expect?
- What do you fear about the future? Are your fears rational or irrational, and do you have any control over the outcome you fear?

APPLY

Whether we admit it or not, we all like to be in control. From deciding whether or not to buy a house to determining at what temperature to set the thermostat, there's nothing too big or too small that we'd like to have our say in.

What does the future hold? We may have plans and hopes and dreams, but the truth is we have little control over what happens today, tomorrow, or a decade from now. Left unchecked, our desire for control can cause sleepless nights or even strife in our relationships, and worry may spiral into despair.

But God, in His infinite wisdom and knowledge of all that has been and all that will be, cares about your future. Even when you are struggling with stress and uncertainty, God is working out your today for a hope-filled tomorrow. Live in His goodness, in His grace, and in His love.

PRAY

God, I give my future to You. Forgive me for acting as if I am in control, because I'm not. You're much better at it. I believe You have good plans for my today and my tomorrows. Align my desires with Your will so that I am living today and every day in You. Please be the Lord of my life, Father. Amen.

You Are Known and Understood

~

Read Psalm 139

KEY VERSES

For you created my inmost being; you knit me together in my mother's womb. I praise you because I am fearfully and wonderfully made; your works are wonderful, I know that full well.

PSALM 139:13–14 NIV

UNDERSTAND

- Who (aside from God) knows you best?
- Think of one thing that makes you unique. Why might your Creator have fashioned you this way?
- Is it important to you that you feel understood? Why?

APPLY

When God created you, He knew you. He didn't need an introduction and time to get to know your quirks and true self. From the moment His artist brush, sculptor hands, and creative mastery formed you, He knew you at the most intimate level. That fact is beautiful and frightening all at once.

On the other hand, we spend so much time creating and wearing masks, conforming to the people and situations around us in order to fit in, to be accepted, to feel normal, that it is a mystery whether we even know ourselves.

Start today by removing your mask. Come before your Creator and loving Father as your true self, the woman He created you to be. Lay your sins, your worries, your regrets, your requests, your heartbreak before Him. He knows you, and He *chooses* to love you, His cherished daughter.

PRAY

Who am I, Father? I've put on so many masks over the years that I'm not sure I know my true self. But You accept me (Romans 15:7), call me Your friend (John 15:15), Your beloved child (Romans 8:17), and You set me free from sin (Galatians 5:1). Today I choose to be known. Reveal Your wisdom to me through Your Word. I want to know You more. Amen.

Where Will You Be at the End of Today?

Read Philippians 3:7–21

KEY VERSES

I focus on this one thing: Forgetting the past and looking forward to what lies ahead, I press on to reach the end of the race and receive the heavenly prize for which God, through Christ Jesus, is calling us.
PHILIPPIANS 3:13–14 NLT

UNDERSTAND

- What can you realistically accomplish today?
- What goals are worthwhile to pursue today? Are there others that aren't worth the time?
- What do you need to forget to allow you to move forward to the future?

APPLY

What's the state of your to-do list? Whether it's a mile long or blessedly under control, life is busy. Stay up late or get up early, we each have only

24 hours a day to get everything done.

There are tasks and responsibilities we must attend to, but the apostle Paul writing to the Philippian church challenges us to focus on the bigger picture—to make it our priority to know Jesus and experience the mighty power that raised Him from the dead.

How can you come closer to that goal today? You're starting out the day right by spending time in His Word and in prayer. Lean on Him throughout the day, and ask Him to guide your steps, your thoughts, your words, and your actions. Commit to seeking Him every morning, taking a step (or a leap) closer to the glory of your brother, Jesus.

Pray

Jesus, I'm forgetting about my past when I struggled to know my true goals from day to day. Now I'm running toward You. Give me the wisdom to continue in that race while I pursue daily responsibilities. I know when I am doing both, my life can and will glorify You! Amen.

Choose to Be a Servant

Read Galatians 5:1-15

KEY VERSE

*For you have been called to live in freedom,
my brothers and sisters. But don't use your
freedom to satisfy your sinful nature. Instead,
use your freedom to serve one another in love.*
GALATIANS 5:13 NLT

UNDERSTAND

- What does freedom mean to you?
- Servants/slaves, by definition, don't have
  complete freedom, yet Paul reminds the
  Galatians that they are free in Christ and
  in the very next sentence tells them to use
  that freedom to serve one another. What
  does this mean to you?

APPLY

The world sees our faith as a list of rules to be
followed—ancient stone tablets filled with "thou
shalts" and—even worse in the world's eyes—the
unending "thou shalt nots" sure to rain on every
parade.

While God's Word does provide guidance in many areas of life along with guardrails to keep us on His perfect path for us, the truth is that the freedom we have because of Jesus' sacrifice gives us unparalleled joy to experience life to the fullest.

One way we can experience that full life is to pour our lives into serving others. Even better, we can follow the example of Jesus by loving our neighbors through our actions. You are free to serve today. Serve your family. Serve your friends. Serve your enemies. It seems counterintuitive, but when we willingly become servants of others, we will experience the true freedom of Christ Jesus.

PRAY

Jesus, today I choose to live in Your freedom. Forgive me for living too often with the shackles of sin around my wrists and ankles by satisfying my own desires. Show me ways to serve and love others today. I am Your willing servant, Lord, who will be Your hands and feet. Amen.

Use Your Words as Building Blocks

Read 1 Thessalonians 5:1–11

KEY VERSE

So encourage each other and build each other up, just as you are already doing.
1 THESSALONIANS 5:11 NLT

UNDERSTAND

- Who encourages you with their words?
- When have you been encouraged at just the right time? What did it mean to you?
- How can you best encourage others with words?

APPLY

Small children know the time it takes to build a tower of blocks and the single moment it takes for a bully to come and knock it down. In a similar way, research shows for every negative message we hear about ourselves, it takes many more positive messages to rebuild confidence. That's just one of the reasons why encouragement is so important.

Your words have power. The words you use to talk, text, and write to others can energize and empower them. The words you use to talk to yourself are just as mighty. Well-used words are building blocks that can construct a fortress of confidence and hope able to withstand the inevitable destruction of criticism and negativity that Satan spews our way.

Today, use encouraging words to build up the people around you. Have a conversation. Send a thoughtful text. Mail a note telling the recipient what they mean to you. Don't wait for signs that someone is struggling and in need of a pick-me-up. The truth is we all need encouragement, and we need it all the time.

Pray

Father God, thank You for Your Word. The Bible as a whole and individual scriptures are such an encouragement to me. Today I am asking You to inhabit my words as I seek to encourage others the way You encourage me. Give me eyes to see those around me as You see them. Amen.

See Others as Jesus Sees Them

∽

Read 1 Samuel 16:1–13

KEY VERSE

*"The LORD doesn't see things the way
you see them. People judge by outward
appearance, but the LORD looks at the heart."*
1 SAMUEL 16:7 NLT

UNDERSTAND

- How does it feel to be judged by what you look like?
- Recall a time when you judged someone else's appearance and were surprised to find out your initial assessment was wrong. What did you learn from that experience?
- Why is the heart more important than physical appearance to God?

APPLY

For those of us blessed with all five senses, sight, sound, smell, taste, and touch help us make sense of our environment. But while these senses can help us understand, experience, and appreciate the temporary, physical world, they don't help us understand the things that are important to God.

The prophet Samuel, sent by God to anoint the next king of Israel, put too much importance on his sense of sight. Surely the tallest, most attractive son of Jesse would be the next king, he thought. God assured Samuel that His interest was not in appearance but in the heart of the individual. And Jesse's youngest, smallest son, David, was the boy for the job.

Today is a day to resist snap judgments based on appearance alone. Do you owe someone a second chance to get to know them? Ask God to show you others through His eyes—straight to the heart.

PRAY

God, I admit that I judge others unfairly. But I also know the unfairness of being judged by my appearance. Give me a beautiful heart overflowing with love, joy, peace, patience, kindness, goodness, faithfulness, and self-control. And if others see any beauty in me, let it be because of You. Amen.

Choose Love Above All

❧

Read 1 John 3:11-20

KEY VERSES

Dear children, let's not merely say that we love each other; let us show the truth by our actions. Our actions will show that we belong to the truth, so we will be confident when we stand before God.

1 JOHN 3:18–19 NLT

UNDERSTAND

- What action, when performed by another, makes you feel most loved? *When they ask for help*
- In what ways (actions) do you show others you love them? *taking people to do the things that need done for themselves*
- How do you best give love? How do you best receive love? *help* *listening to me*

APPLY

Our Father God shows us He loves us in so many ways. His Word tells us of His love and devotion for us. He listens to our prayers. He provides for our needs. And Jesus Christ became the very definition of love by laying down

His life to make a way for each of us to be with Him for eternity.

So, when John encourages us to go beyond just saying that we love each other, he tells us to display the truth of our words by putting love into action. Love displayed in multiple, tangible ways empowers relationships and makes us stronger together.

Who do you need to show some love to today? Don't let opportunities slip by for showing love in action. Love, in the name of God, is life-giving truth that can sustain us in the hardest times.

PRAY

Jesus, when I feel self-conscious and ill-equipped to show love in action, remind me of Your astounding act of humility on the cross. You showed me how to love perfectly, and I want to follow Your example. Put opportunities to love in my path today, Lord. My heart is open, and my hands are ready to do Your will. Amen.

Guard Your Heart

❧

Read Proverbs 4

KEY VERSE

Above all else, guard your heart,
for everything you do flows from it.
PROVERBS 4:23 NIV

UNDERSTAND

- What does it mean to guard your heart?
- Describe a time when you let your heart guard down. What were the results?
- Why do you think the writer of Proverbs put such high value on guarding the heart rather than the head or the emotions?

APPLY

We've all been through seasons of heartsickness. It's that deep feeling of disappointment when we lose someone or something. A relationship. A loved one. A job. A pet. An opportunity that we'd set our hopes on. At the onset of heartsickness, it feels like nothing will ever be normal again. We can't see past the loss, the failure, the disappointment, and the what-ifs. Even with our faith intact, heartsickness is a tough slog.

Most of Proverbs 4 is all about seeking after wisdom—about walking on the path of righteousness and avoiding the pitfalls of evil. These are all good and right. But the heart—a healthy heart—is the key "for everything you do flows from it" (v. 23 NIV).

Need a heart check-up? Spend time seeking God this morning. Ask the Holy Spirit to come alive in your heart, and He will be your guard and guide no matter what comes your way.

PRAY

Holy Spirit, come alive in my heart now. Help me to feel Your presence as I start my day. Turn my heart toward the things that are important to the Father, and guard against the people and situations that can lead to heartsickness. Create in me a pure heart concerned with God's glory. Amen.

Mind Control

❧

Read Romans 8:1–8

KEY VERSE

So letting your sinful nature control your mind leads to death. But letting the Spirit control your mind leads to life and peace.
ROMANS 8:6 NLT

UNDERSTAND

- How do you know your sinful nature is rearing its head for control of your mind?
- How do you know the Holy Spirit is controlling your mind?
- How could your day be different if you allowed the Spirit full control?

APPLY

For most of us, our minds are in overdrive even before our feet hit the floor in the morning. Our brains are so jam-packed with schedules and responsibilities and to-do lists that we barely have time to think about anything outside of what must be done—now.

But even with an overloaded mind, there

are still negative feelings or harsh criticisms or resentful feelings or spite or even lustful fantasies that barge in. These thought patterns are all evidence that our sinful nature is in control, and Romans 8 tells us that leads to death when left unchecked.

But that's not the end! Life and peace are there for each of us when we let the Holy Spirit control our minds. How? Right now, first thing this morning, surrender your mind to God's perfect will. Ask for His guidance. And continue to give your mind over to the Spirit throughout the day. He is faithful to supply life-giving thoughts, grounded in the love of God.

PRAY

God, I'm done giving my sinful nature control of my mind. Today I choose to surrender my thoughts and feelings to Your will. I invite the Holy Spirit to take the helm of my mind. I know with You in control, I will live a peaceful life filled with Your promises. Amen.

Guard Your Tongue

Read James 3:1–12

Key Verse

For if we could control our tongues,
we would be perfect and could also
control ourselves in every other way.

James 3:2 NLT

Understand

- In what situations are you most likely to lose control of your tongue?
- James likens the tongue to a flame of fire (James 3:6). When have you seen words create devastation like an out-of-control fire?
- When have you held your tongue despite wanting to say something? How did it make you feel?

Apply

If you're doing this study early in the morning, maybe you haven't had a chance to open mouth, insert foot yet—the day is still young. James 3:8 tells us that unlike all kinds of animals, birds, reptiles, and fish that can be trained and tamed, no one can tame the tongue.

So, if we can't tame it, we must keep it under lock and key.

Proverbs 21:23 (ESV) tells us "Whoever keeps his mouth and his tongue keeps himself out of trouble." Psalm 34:13 (NLT) says to "Keep your tongue from speaking evil and your lips from telling lies!" God has given us speech for a reason, and from our words can come encouraging, life-giving hope. But we must learn to listen first, consider second, and answer (when necessary) third. Ask God for the words He would have you say (or not say), and He will help you use your words wisely.

PRAY

Father, only You can help me get a handle on this powerful muscle in my mouth. My tongue gets me into trouble too often, but I also admit that I too often react with my tongue. Give me the wisdom to know when and what to speak and when to remain silent. Amen.

Stop and Think

∽

Read Ephesians 4:25–32

Key Verse

"Don't sin by letting anger control you."
Don't let the sun go down while
you are still angry.
Ephesians 4:26 NLT

Understand

- What people or situations automatically get your hackles up?
- Have you ever been so angry that you felt out of control of your words, actions, or thoughts? What was the outcome?
- What practical safeguards can you take to remain silent and think when you are getting angry?

Apply

When anger rises, you may not *literally* see red, but we all know that feeling. Maybe you're reacting to a careless word said by another or an injustice that must be righted. Or it could be good, old-fashioned road rage. The kids are fighting. . .again. The dog eviscerated a new pair of shoes. Your husband did the thing that irritates you more than you like to admit. And here comes that blood-rushing, pulse-pounding, face-flushing, frustration-spiking wave of emotion called anger.

When anger comes—and it *will* come—you have a choice: explode in an emotion-fueled reaction or simply stop and think.

Simple? Yes. Easy? Not at all. But the Creator of our complex emotions understands anger, and He also knows such a strong emotion can lead us to sinful actions, words, and thoughts. So, train your mind, heart, and tongue to stop, give control to the Holy Spirit, and then, at His prompting, react in love.

PRAY

Jesus, sometimes giving in to anger in the moment just feels good. But I also know the destruction in the wake of an angry outburst is hard to clean up. I've hurt people I love in the past, and that's the last thing I want to do in the future. Give me wisdom to stop and think before reacting in anger today. Amen.

Avoiding Gossip

Read Proverbs 26:17–28

KEY VERSE

Fire goes out without wood, and quarrels disappear when gossip stops.
PROVERBS 26:20 NLT

UNDERSTAND

- Do you find gossip hard to avoid? Why or why not?
- Have you ever been the subject of gossip? How did it make you feel when you found out?
- The Bible uses the metaphor of fire for our tongue and destructive words we speak. What do words and fire have in common?

APPLY

Proverbs 26 is chock-full of relational wisdom. From the pitfalls of lying and butting into others' disagreements to warnings against flattery and smooth talking, the overarching message of this chapter is clear: it's often best to mind your own business.

Engaging in gossip—talking about someone behind their back—is the epitome of *not* minding your own business, and it can lead to misunderstanding, broken trust, and damaged relationships. Ah, but those bits of newsy gossip are so delicious, aren't they? Verse 22 (NLT) describes rumors as "dainty morsels that sink deep into one's heart" for good reason.

If you've developed an appetite for gossip, sometimes the easiest and simplest way to kick the habit is to avoid conversations with the person or people who are gossiping. If that's not possible, ask God for the wisdom to tell the others nibbling at the rumor morsels with you that you will no longer engage in it.

PRAY

Father, I never meant to gossip. It started out innocent enough. A "concern" of a mutual friend masqueraded as a prayer request, and it grew from there. Now feelings are hurt, and I feel terrible. So, I will keep my mouth shut, and Your Word says the fighting will disappear. I'm holding tightly to that truth, God! Amen.

1/1

A New You

Read 2 Corinthians 5:11–21

Key Verse

Therefore, if anyone is in Christ, he is a new creation. The old has passed away; behold, the new has come.

2 Corinthians 5:17 ESV

Understand

Not to be grateful what I have than n

- In what ways do you try to change yourself for the better? Physically? Mentally? ASK for g Emotionally? Spiritually? for him and I to bec
- Many fairy tales deal with transformation (Cinderella, the Little Mermaid). Why do these stories resonate with us at any age?

Becoming one with the father and god one is possible with him

Apply

There's something thrilling about an extreme transformation. From a professional makeover to a weight loss in the triple digits, we cheer for the individuals in these stories as they seek to change themselves for the better. To gain more confidence. To get healthier. Their improved selves are revealed, and they often are empowered by the change.

These kinds of physical changes are well and good, but they aren't eternal. Only God can truly transform us into new creations, perfectly forgiven because of the sacrifice of Jesus on the cross. Our old, sinful selves *die*. We are no longer who or what we were, and God's great mystery of new creation happens. We're not a better version of ourselves, we are made *new*. And whole. And perfectly loved.

Have you grasped fully the fact that you are new, sister? You aren't used, washed up, or a second-hand treasure. Your new self is *here* now. Today, celebrate your newness in Christ!

PRAY

Thank You, Lord, for making me new. You did not leave me in my own sinfulness, and You have such abundant life for me to live out as Your loved child. I want to live each day in eager anticipation of new experiences with You. Draw me close, Father. Continue to make me more like You. I long for continued transformation! Amen.

Arm Yourself for Today's Battles

Read Ephesians 6:10–20

KEY VERSE

Therefore put on the full armor of God, so that when the day of evil comes, you may be able to stand your ground, and after you have done everything, to stand.
EPHESIANS 6:13 NIV

UNDERSTAND

- How have you seen the armor of God be helpful to you both spiritually and in practical, everyday life?
- Which piece of the armor of God is the easiest for you to take up? Which is the most challenging? Why?

APPLY

You are powerful. Why? Because the Spirit of God lives inside you. And God has given us tools to meet life's challenges head-on with the armor of God.

So, what are you facing today? When Satan

whispers his lies that you aren't good enough, tighten the belt of God's truth around your waist and know that you are cherished and loved. Guard your heart with the breastplate of righteousness, and stand firm in the peace of the Gospel that Jesus came to earth to make a way for us to live with Him forever. Hold high that shield of faith that gives you hope even in hard times. Secure your helmet of salvation, and rest in the knowledge that you cannot lose God's saving grace. Grip tightly the hilt of the sword of the Spirit—your counterattack when Satan does his worst. And when you've done all you can today, stand, knowing that God wins every battle.

PRAY

Almighty God, I am not a fierce warrior, but Your Spirit makes me strong. When Satan charges at me, give me Your fearless bravery and the security to know that the power of Your Holy Spirit inside me has already prevailed over every kind of evil. I trust You, Father. Amen.

By God's Side

Read Psalm 73

KEY VERSE

*But as for me, it is good to be near God.
I have made the Sovereign LORD my
refuge; I will tell of all your deeds.*
PSALM 73:28 NIV

UNDERSTAND

- When is it most difficult for you to feel near to God?
- When is it easiest for you to feel near to God?
- What is God doing in your life now? Who can you tell about it?

APPLY

The writer of Psalm 73 is going through a hard time. All around him, he sees evil people prospering. While he struggles and wrestles with his faith and daily life, he sees wicked people living a carefree existence. And he's angry about it. Why would God make the lives of bad people *easy* while His chosen people work endlessly to keep a pure heart, doing the Lord's work?

Maybe you've felt this way. *What's all this work for*, you wonder, *when other people are living it up and having a much better life than I am?*

Don't give up. God is here, and just like the psalm writer, realize that His nearness is a blessed refuge to the challenges of life. Give Him your frustrations—He can take it. Lean into Him in quiet time, Bible study, and prayer. Remember His faithfulness in the past. Celebrate His devotion to you today. Look forward to His (and your) victory tomorrow and forever.

PRAY

God, I am here with You, and You are here with me. Make Your presence so real that I cannot deny that I am by Your side. Please give me a glimpse into Your plan, especially when I see situations that I simply do not understand. I long to understand what You are doing behind the scenes. I trust You, Father. Amen.

You Are Never Alone

Read John 14:15-26

KEY VERSES

"And I will ask the Father, and he will give you another Helper, to be with you forever, even the Spirit of truth, whom the world cannot receive, because it neither sees him nor knows him. You know him, for he dwells with you and will be in you."

JOHN 14:16–17 ESV

UNDERSTAND

- What does the Holy Spirit mean to you?
- Does the Spirit ever seem dormant inside you? Why do you think that is?
- What is one practical way you can engage with the Holy Spirit today?

APPLY

Jesus' disciples must've felt panicked. Their beloved Rabbi had said repeatedly He would soon leave them. And if He was sincere in His promise, what would they do without Him? He is the Son of God who guided them on the path of truth, answered their questions, challenged them, and comforted them.

They couldn't understand it then, but the Helper that Jesus promised His Father would send would be so much more. Jesus came to earth to be God with us. The Spirit arrived to be God *in* us. Think of it! The same almighty, powerful God who spoke the world into existence has taken a home in your heart. . .forever!

You are not alone. You cannot be separated from God's love no more than you can be separated from His Spirit. Don't let this magnificent Helper go unnoticed today! Breathe in the Spirit, and ask for help to live out God's plan today.

PRAY

Spirit of God, sometimes You are a mystery to me. But I long to know You better. Come alive in my heart today and make Your presence known. Jesus said You are my Helper. So, I am asking for Your help. Help me even when I act like I don't need it. Amen.

You Have the Peace of Jesus

∾

Read John 14:27-31

KEY VERSE

"Peace I leave with you.
My peace I give to you."
JOHN 14:27 NLV

UNDERSTAND

- How is the peace of Jesus different than what the world defines as peace?
- Can fear and peace exist at the same time? Why or why not?
- What areas of your life need peace today?

APPLY

The world defines peace as the absence of war, but as Christians, we know that the peace of Jesus is so much more than that. Within the holy peace of God lies faith that He is in control of every circumstance; trust that He works all things for the good of those who love Him; hope, especially in the midst of difficult situations; and a deep contentment rooted in the joy of the Lord.

How do we experience this peace? It comes down to surrender. We must allow Jesus to be the Lord of every aspect of our lives. When we no longer hold tightly to the control of our desires, our relationships, and our wishes and dreams and instead ask Jesus to guide our steps, that's when real peace takes hold. We realize it's not all on our shoulders.

Breathe in, breathe out. Accept the peace that Jesus offers.

PRAY

Savior, Your peace is what I long for. This morning, fill me with the deep restfulness and contentment that only You can offer. When I try to take back control, gently remind me that the only way to peace is to let it go. Make me an instrument of Your peace to everyone around me today, and energize me as I walk the path You lay before me. Amen.

No Complaints

Read Philippians 2:12–18

KEY VERSES

Do all things without grumbling or disputing,
that you may be blameless and innocent,
children of God without blemish in the midst
of a crooked and twisted generation, among
whom you shine as lights in the world.
PHILIPPIANS 2:14–16 ESV

UNDERSTAND

- How would your life be different if you did all things without grumbling?
- What is one thing you find yourself complaining about?
- Instead of complaining, how could you take your dissatisfaction and turn it into something positive?

APPLY

Do you know anyone who has the gift of complaining? Instigators, party poopers, wet blankets, and Debbie Downers alike, these individuals bring down the mood with one well-placed criticism or grumble. Unfortunately, it's easier for a complainer to pull others down into their own mire than it is for others to raise them up to a more optimistic outlook.

As followers of Jesus, we are called to be better rather than bitter. And when we adopt the attitude of Christ and choose to neither complain nor argue, others will see something special and attractive in us. We'll shine brightly the love of God in a world dimmed by dissatisfaction, petty grumbling, and strife. When people ask what makes us different, we can point them straight to the love of Jesus.

Choose today to do *everything* without complaining and see how your outlook changes!

Pray

God, I'm guilty of whining when I should be praising You for Your endless goodness to me. Forgive me. I want to be Your blameless and innocent daughter who can point others to Your love. Take away any discontentment and bitterness in my heart and replace it with Your joy. Amen.

You Are Part of Christ's Body

Read 1 Corinthians 12:12–26

KEY VERSES

So God has put the body together such that extra honor and care are given to those parts that have less dignity. This makes for harmony among the members, so that all the members care for each other. If one part suffers, all the parts suffer with it, and if one part is honored, all the parts are glad.

1 CORINTHIANS 12:24–26 NLT

UNDERSTAND

- How can you tell when your church is a healthy body of Christ?
- When have you experienced harmony among the members of the body of Christ?
- How have you been cared for by your church family?

APPLY

Life for the Christian isn't meant to be an individual or private faith. Yes, we are made to be in a relationship with our Father God, but we live in this world together with other believers. Before Jesus returned to heaven, He established His Church—what Paul describes in 1 Corinthians 12 as the body of Christ.

You are a unique part of your church, made with talents and passions and gifts, and you are cast in a role that only you can play. Body parts must work together and compensate when one part struggles, as well as celebrate and reap the benefits when one part is successful.

How's the health of your church as a whole? Are you doing life together, unified in faith? What practical steps can you take today to get involved in the lives of others?

PRAY

Jesus, I am thankful for my church. We are Your body, made up of flawed individuals, but You bind us together in unity, and we are better for it. Forgive me when I wrongly believe I am better on my own. Amen.

Be Yourself

Read Matthew 6:5-13

KEY VERSES

*"When you pray, do not be as those who
pretend to be someone they are not. They
love to stand and pray in the places of worship
or in the streets so people can see them. . . .
When you pray, go into a room by yourself.
After you have shut the door, pray to your
Father Who is in secret. Then your Father
Who sees in secret will reward you."*

MATTHEW 6:5-6 NLV

UNDERSTAND

- Why might someone be tempted to
  try to sound more spiritual than they
  really are?
- Do you use different words when you
  pray in public than when you pray
  silently? Why or why not?

APPLY

God doesn't require eloquent speech, complete
sentences, or even coherent thoughts in prayer.

He wants to hear from your authentic self, speaking intimately and from your heart.

If you get the opportunity to pray aloud in public, be sure that your prayer motives are pure. God doesn't want a show, and He doesn't want you to pretend to be someone you aren't. In these instances, others—especially children—may look to you as an example of how to pray, and the best example you can set is one of a pure heart with a singular desire to connect with your heavenly Father.

Practice being authentic in prayer behind closed doors, and that authenticity will flow into other areas. Be yourself—perfectly loved and forgiven by God.

Pray

Father, I come before You this morning with no motive other than to be in Your presence. I am not pretending to be better than I am. I admit that I have no answers. I realize that I can't do life today without You. I need You, God. Please be near, and never leave me. Amen.

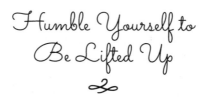

Humble Yourself to Be Lifted Up

Read Philippians 2:1-11

KEY VERSES

Don't be selfish; don't try to impress others. Be humble, thinking of others as better than yourselves. Don't look out only for your own interests, but take an interest in others, too.

PHILIPPIANS 2:3-4 NLT

UNDERSTAND

- Other than Jesus, who is the humblest person you know?
- What is the biggest challenge you face in living a life of humility?
- What is the difference between humility and weakness?

APPLY

If we're honest with ourselves, we probably care entirely too much what other people think of us. From an early age, we're told to aim to be the best. To achieve. To win. To look out for ourselves first, our loved ones second, and everyone else can worry about themselves.

But the kingdom of God is different than this world. In fact, in many ways it's an upside-down kingdom where the greatest among us are the most humble, the most giving. They're the ones who lay aside their own wishes to bring glory to God. And in the case of Jesus, He gave up everything—including His very life—to complete God's perfect will for humankind.

Today, intentionally put others ahead of yourself. See them as God sees them, and honor each person you encounter as His child. God will honor your humility and lift you up.

PRAY

Jesus, thank You for showing me the way to humility. When I think I am better than others, remind me of what You did on earth. You lived humbly, with no place to call home. You gave up everything for me. I cannot repay You for that, but I will offer my life as a humble offering to You. Amen.

Choose to Live in Grace

Read Romans 6:1-14

KEY VERSE

*For sin shall no longer be your master, because
you are not under the law, but under grace.*
ROMANS 6:14 NIV

UNDERSTAND

- How did your life change from the time that
  sin was your master to living under God's
  grace?
- What tricks does Satan use to make you
  think you are still under the control of your
  sinful desires?
- What does God's grace mean to you?

APPLY

The world defines freedom as doing whatever
we want when we want. It's doing what feels
good, what feels right at the time. But while our
own evil desires may masquerade as ultimate
freedom, sin is really the cruelest of slave
masters.

Jesus came to offer us *true* freedom from the

bondage of sin. And through His death, burial, and resurrection, Paul tells us in Romans 6:6 (NIV) that "our old self was crucified with him so that the body ruled by sin might be done away with, that we should no longer be slaves to sin."

Sin has a sneaky way of looking for a crack and snaking its way back into our lives. Before we know it, a new sin stronghold has taken root. Examine your heart today. You are free from that cruel slave master! Break free of the chains and live in grace!

PRAY

Jesus, I long to be free of the sin that so easily pops up in my life. Old habits are hard to break, but I know that Your power is stronger than any temptation I can face. Help me to live confidently in Your grace, today and every day. And help me to extend that grace to others who have yet to know You. Amen.

You Are Blessed to Be a Blessing

Read 2 Corinthians 9:6–15

KEY VERSE

You will be enriched in every way so that you can be generous on every occasion, and through us your generosity will result in thanksgiving to God.

2 CORINTHIANS 9:11 NIV

UNDERSTAND

- Why does God bless you?
- When have you been the recipient of someone's generosity? What did it mean to you?
- What needs can you meet today?

APPLY

We ask for and eagerly welcome God's blessings into our lives—food, shelter, clothing, money, to name a few—but why does God provide us with these things? One reason is that He enjoys giving good gifts to His children (see Matthew 7:11 and James 1:17), but another reason explained in 2 Corinthians 9 is that God blesses us so we can be a blessing to others.

Think of it! God gives us the opportunity to pay forward the good gifts He gives to us. He invites us to follow His example and give generously, which not only blesses the receiver but enriches our lives and results in praise and thanks to God!

Be on the lookout for ways to be generous with your time, talent, and money. And in the meantime, prepare to be generous. Make time to do it. Save money to do it. God is blessing you—to be a blessing!

PRAY

Lord God, You are so good to me! Today I am not taking for granted everything You give to me. I am so blessed! Show me where You want me to be generous today. Keep my motives pure and my eyes open to Your will. My desire is for Your blessings to not stop here but flow through me. Amen.

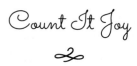

Count It Joy

Read James 1:2-18

KEY VERSES

Count it all joy. . .when you meet trials of various kinds, for you know that the testing of your faith produces steadfastness. And let steadfastness have its full effect, that you may be perfect and complete, lacking in nothing.
JAMES 1:2-4 ESV

UNDERSTAND

- Does the promise of a stronger faith after enduring trials make it easier to endure them? Why or why not?
- What difficulties have you come through that resulted in a greater faith?
- How can you encourage someone who is going through a hard time?

APPLY

It's easy to live a joyful life when the birds are singing, there's a spring in your step, and all is right with the world.

But this is real life, and if those carefree

seasons come, they are woefully short-lived.

James encourages us to count every difficulty, every bump in the road, and every dead end a joy. Why? Because challenges, frustrations, and disappointments grow our faith and dependence on God. He will strengthen you through anything life can throw at you and your family; and when you emerge on the other side, James says your faith will be greater, more perfect, and complete.

Are you in a difficult season now? Hold on, don't give up, and find joy in the fact that God is working. He will bring you through to a better tomorrow.

PRAY

*Almighty Father, I long to experience
Your joy. But it is hard to be joyful when
everything is so difficult right now. Help me
to look past the challenges of today to see
what You're doing in my life and in my current
situation. I love You and I trust You. Amen.*

Work with Your Whole Heart

❧

Read Colossians 3:18–25

KEY VERSE

*Work willingly at whatever you do,
as though you were working for
the Lord rather than for people.*
COLOSSIANS 3:23 NLT

UNDERSTAND

- When is it easiest for you to work willingly?
- When is it difficult for you to work willingly?
- What must change for you to work willingly and put forward your best effort in every situation?

APPLY

Some tasks are easy, fulfilling, and give us great satisfaction to see them completed. Other tasks are impossible, frustrating, and leave us feeling drained. Some bosses are motivating, encouraging, and kind. Other bosses are demanding, critical, and harsh.

God doesn't make a distinction between any of these scenarios. His Word tells us to work willingly at whatever is asked of us, knowing that our work in His name is important and necessary and holy and is a blessing in our lives and in the lives of others.

If you're unconvinced that your role in your job, at home with your family, in your volunteer work, or in your ministry can make a difference, consider this: if you surrender your work to God and give it your best effort for His glory, He will bless your work beyond what you could imagine. Roll up your sleeves—the Lord's work needs to be done!

PRAY

Lord God, I give my job to You. I give my role in my family to You. I give every task and responsibility to You. Bless my boss and the other leaders I work with and for. Let me be an encouragement to them and to others around me. I want to be Your light wherever I am. Amen.

Master Your Time

～

Read Ephesians 5:15–20

KEY VERSES

Make the most of every opportunity in these evil days. Don't act thoughtlessly, but understand what the Lord wants you to do.
EPHESIANS 5:16–17 NLT

UNDERSTAND

- What do you think Ephesians 5:16 means when it tells you to "make the most of every opportunity"?
- Do you consider yourself a good time manager? Why or why not?
- What motivates you to act now when you'd rather procrastinate? *my goals*

APPLY

In the 21st century, we've become expert time wasters. From bingeworthy TV, Pinterest, and video games to social media, Internet research rabbit holes, and photo filters, we're willing to let just about any distraction occupy our time—often while avoiding the important things we *should* be doing.

We may treat time like it's an inexhaustible resource, but the truth is our life on earth is fleeting, and that's why Paul in Ephesians 5 is urging us to take hold of opportunities when they arise. The psalmist also understood the urgency when he wrote, "Teach us to understand how many days we have. Then we will have a heart of wisdom to give You" (Psalm 90:12 NLV).

Today, choose the wise path and use your time wisely. Seize opportunities to love others. Spend less thoughtless time staring at your phone and look up. Ask God how He wants you to spend your time. A 24-hour day spent in the Lord's work goes a lot further than does the same amount of time spent scrolling through social media or bingeing a show.

PRAY

Father, forgive me for wasting Your gift of time. Give me the wisdom to be busy in Your work, moving toward goals that further Your kingdom and draw others closer to You. Make my times of rest holy and refreshing so I can continue to give You my best. Amen.

Choose to Be Free

∽

Read John 8:31-47

KEY VERSE

*"So if the Son sets you free,
you will be free indeed."*

JOHN 8:36 NIV

UNDERSTAND

with their heart
their
Love

- In what ways does the world tell us we can find freedom? How are these flawed?
- What is keeping you from experiencing the complete freedom that Jesus offers?

*helping others that don't
want to help them selfs*

APPLY

Under Old Testament law, there existed a way to be right with God, but even the most righteous could not follow every rule. The way to freedom was shackled with unachievable requirements.

Without Jesus, sin had a death grip on each of us. Our own selfish desires and destructive habits and thought patterns kept us oppressed, fearful, and clinging to our own filth because, we thought, at least it was *our* filth, and we were comfortable in it, even if that meant we were a slave to it.

But that false sense of comfort was and still is a lie from Satan, and the life-giving truth of Jesus is the only way to break free of the death grip of sin. "Now a slave has no permanent place in the family, but a son belongs to it forever," Jesus said in John 8:35 (NIV). You are a beloved child of God, dear to Him and an important part of His family.

Today, Jesus has set you free. Grasp on to the truth of your worth, your value, the preciousness of your salvation, and be free!

PRAY

Jesus, fill me with Your truth today so that I may live in real freedom. I admit that I too often return to my own filth and selfish desires, and sometimes I start to feel sin's death grip try to take hold again. Forgive me. I am here, standing in the love of our Father as Your sister and friend. Amen.

Daily Purity

Read 1 John 1:5-10

KEY VERSE

If we confess our sins, he is faithful and just and will forgive us our sins and purify us from all unrighteousness.

1 JOHN 1:9 NIV

UNDERSTAND

- Why is it important that God offers us forgiveness time and time again?
- Are you ever tempted to deny that you've sinned at all? What is the result?
- How does forgiveness feel on a heart level?

APPLY

We Christians talk a lot about forgiveness and rightfully so. God's forgiveness and grace are essential to our faith and salvation. But God's forgiveness is a bigger concept than simply pardoning our sin. The forgiveness available to us through the blood of Jesus Christ purifies us just as if we had never sinned in the first place, leaving us holy, righteous, and blameless in the sight of God.

God's perfect forgiveness offers us purity. It makes us without blemish and whole. Because of that, we can stand confident before the King of kings and Lord of lords. These are the things we stand to gain when we humble ourselves and confess our sins to God. Confession leads to transformation as we grow to be more like Christ. There's no other way to start again, to join Him in the light of His goodness.

Start today in confession. Admit where you've failed. God is listening, and He will purify you again.

PRAY

Father, I come before You this morning seeking Your forgiveness. I messed up. . .again. My sin creates a divide between You and me, and I can't bear it. Although I feel unworthy to ask You to do it again, please purify my heart. Cover me in Your grace and make me righteous before You. Amen.

God's Good Creation

~

Read Psalm 19:1-6

KEY VERSE

*The heavens are telling of the greatness
of God and the great open spaces
above show the work of His hands.*

PSALM 19:1 NLV

UNDERSTAND

- When has God's creation awed you so
  much that you couldn't help but worship?
- What does God's creation reveal to you
  about His character? His aesthetic
  preferences?
- What one thing do you think is most
  interesting or fascinating in all of God's
  creation?

APPLY

Our God delights in transformation. From the
caterpillar changing to the butterfly to the sea-
sonal cycles of the leaves of deciduous trees,
creation constantly changes according to His
masterful plan. The sky—what Psalm 19 refers

to as "the heavens"—may be the best example of constant change. Consider how the sunrise's Creator uses different palettes of color and varying brush strokes each day to fill the sky with beauty. And the night sky is no different as God directs the moon's phases and lights up the vast expanse with innumerable pieces of light.

The heavens say so much about God's greatness without using a single word.

Today, really look at God's creation. Raise your eyes to the sky. Kneel to be eye level with a child. Notice a flower or a bird's song or a dog's bark. He created our world—including you—for His pleasure and for our blessing.

PRAY

Creator God, today I am celebrating Your artistry throughout all of Your creation. Even in nature around me every day, I can learn much about You. Give me Your eyes to appreciate and delight in the things You delight in. I praise You for the Master Artist You are. You have made all things good and pleasing in Your sight. Amen.

All Things

Read Romans 8:18-30

KEY VERSE

We know that God makes all things work together for the good of those who love Him and are chosen to be a part of His plan.
ROMANS 8:28 NLV

UNDERSTAND

- How does Romans 8:28 give you hope?
- Do you trust that God has good in store for you? Why or why not?
- What are you hopefully waiting for that you do not have now (see Romans 8:24)?

APPLY

Romans 8:28 ranks high on the list of verses that Christians commit to memory. You may have learned it as a song when you were a child or written it on an index card to remember the hope it carries: no matter what, God makes *all things* work together for the good of His children.

Not some things. Not just the easy things.

Not just the good things. All things. The hard things. The heartbreaking things. The frustrating things. The moments when it seems like nothing good can come, God is working it for our good.

The unspoken part of Romans 8:28 is that we're often waiting while He is working. And waiting is hard. But waiting with the promise of this verse brings hope. What are you hoping for today? Ask God to reveal His work to you as you wait. He is faithful to deliver on His promises in His time.

PRAY

Good, good Father, thank You for the hope of Your promise that You're working all things together for my good. When I don't understand what You are doing, it's hard for me to wait, but still I hope. And I know my hope in You is never in vain. Give me patience to wait on Your timing and Your plan. Amen.

He Is Always Kind

Read Titus 3:3–8

KEY VERSES

When God our Savior revealed his kindness and love, he saved us, not because of the righteous things we had done, but because of his mercy. He washed away our sins, giving us a new birth and new life through the Holy Spirit.

TITUS 3:4–5 NLT

UNDERSTAND

- How have you tried to earn God's favor?
- Why is trying to earn God's favor a futile endeavor?

APPLY

Of all the characteristics of God, His kindness toward us is one that we should praise Him for every day. Kindness seems like such a simple thing, but it goes hand-in-hand with His passionate love for His children. His kindness allows us to approach Him when we know we've messed up. His care for us helps us to be confident that He will not condemn us in our sin when we sincerely repent and ask for forgiveness. His kindness was what resulted in His plan for our salvation through Jesus Christ.

We can't earn His kindness. He cannot be kinder to us or love us more if we say the right things or act a certain way. He loves us so much that He offers us new life in the Holy Spirit.

Your kind Father is waiting to hear from you. What is on your heart today that you'd like to tell Him? He will not judge you. He will respond in love. . .and in kindness.

PRAY

Father, when I think of all the ways You demonstrate how You love me, I realize just how kind You are to me. You bless me in so many ways, and You give me an identity in Christ that is perfect and whole—not dependent on my own goodness or abilities. Give me opportunities to show Your kindness to others today. Amen.

You Are Chosen by Christ

❧

Read John 15:1-17

KEY VERSE

*"You didn't choose me. I chose you.
I appointed you to go and produce
lasting fruit, so that the Father will give
you whatever you ask for, using my name."*
JOHN 15:16 NLT

UNDERSTAND

- Jesus didn't *have* to choose you; He *decided* to choose you. What does that mean to you?
- Jesus calls His followers His friends in John 15:14. How does friendship with Jesus affect how you think of your relationship with Him?

APPLY

We've all felt the sting of rejection. Whether we're overlooked by peers, passed over for a promotion, or have been abandoned by a friend, insecurities we think we've long laid to rest can resurface in a moment. And we feel useless. Unworthy. Like a failure. Less than others.

Sister, Jesus Christ chooses you.

Today you stand in the love of Christ, who handpicked you before you were born to be His friend. You belong in His family. He invites you to experience the fullness of His Father's kingdom. All you need do is, in turn, remain in His love. Follow Him, obey His commandments, and experience the overflowing joy He offers today. Pray confidently in the name of Jesus, and align your heart to God's wondrous plan for your life.

You are appointed by Christ today. You are chosen. You are loved.

PRAY

Jesus, "thank You" seems inadequate for my gratitude that You have chosen me. When others have turned their backs, I am confident that You never will. You are the vine, and I am the branch, and I will remain in You all my days. Thank You for remaining steadfast to the work of the Father. Amen.

You Are Strong in the Lord

2 Corinthians 12:1-10

KEY VERSES

Each time he said, "My grace is all you need.
My power works best in weakness." So now
I am glad to boast about my weaknesses, so
that the power of Christ can work through me.
That's why I take pleasure in my weaknesses,
and in the insults, hardships, persecutions,
and troubles that I suffer for Christ. For
when I am weak, then I am strong.
2 CORINTHIANS 12:9-10 NLT

UNDERSTAND

- Why does Paul admit to weakness in this passage?
- What challenges do you have that only God can overcome?

APPLY

The apostle Paul is a giant of our Christian faith. This man with a miraculous conversion story (see Acts 9) went on to preach the Gospel, greatly encourage congregations to the ends of the earth, and pen thirteen of the books in the New Testament. By anyone's standards, Paul had much to boast about.

But here in 2 Corinthians 12, Paul downplays his accomplishments and instead focuses on his own weaknesses. We don't know what his specific difficulty was, but it was something that he could only overcome with God's help. And God's strength, Paul says, is best displayed through human weakness.

Where are your weaknesses, your struggles? Whether it's something physical, spiritual, mental, or emotional, turn it over to God. With the power of the Holy Spirit inside of you, His strength will be made perfect in your weakness.

PRAY

God, when this world tells me to be empowered by my own strength, remind me that I am nothing without You. It feels strange to say it, but I thank You for my weak spots. Fill those gaps with Your power, dear Lord, and I will be strong in You today and forever. Amen.

You Can Resist Temptation

Read 1 Corinthians 10:12-31

KEY VERSES

If you think you are standing strong, be careful not to fall. The temptations in your life are no different from what others experience. And God is faithful. He will not allow the temptation to be more than you can stand. When you are tempted, he will show you a way out so that you can endure.

1 CORINTHIANS 10:12-13 NLT

UNDERSTAND

- Do you think the temptations you face are different from others? Why or why not?
- Why is it dangerous to think you are too strong to fall to temptation?

APPLY

Temptations come in many forms. Sin-inducing desires happen to everyone—even or especially to the strongest Christians—so that's why the apostle Paul tells us to be careful and realize no one is above falling to temptation.

But, he goes on to say, others have resisted temptation, and so can we because God is faithful to help us stand firm and not give in. Ask Him to show you the people and situations that give you trouble. Ask Him to help you run from anything you know is wrong and choose to do only what is right. Earnestly ask for His help, and seek friends who love God and can offer support when you are tempted.

Paul tells us that our Father will not allow our temptations to be more than we can stand. Today, stand firm in that promise of God's faithfulness.

PRAY

God, I know when I am tempted to sin that temptation doesn't come from You— it comes from my own selfish desires. Help me to recognize the areas in which I am most vulnerable to temptation, and deliver on Your promise that You will show me an exit to avoid the temptation. Amen.

You Can Choose Joy

Read Psalm 118

KEY VERSE

This is the day the LORD has made.
We will rejoice and be glad in it.
PSALM 118:24 NLT

UNDERSTAND

- What are some of the difficulties written about in Psalm 118?
- Why do you think the psalmist still chooses to praise God?
- How can you rejoice in today even if you are going through a hard season?

APPLY

Psalm 118 starts and ends in the same way: "Give thanks to the LORD, for he is good! His faithful love endures forever" (vv. 1, 29 NLT). This statement of praise and appreciation for God bookends a chapter filled with great challenges and great victories. Through hostility and attacks from enemies, the psalm writer continues to come back to the fact that God is the Rescuer, that He hears and answers prayer, that He puts purpose and joy in each day.

What if you started and ended your day in joyful appreciation for what God is doing? "Thank You, Lord, for being so good to me. Your faithful love endures forever!" This morning, set the stage for rejoicing in today, and tonight, before you lay your head on the pillow, thank Him again. Rejoice and be glad in today, knowing that God is working all things together for your good (see Romans 8:28)!

PRAY

God, today I am choosing joy. Not because everything is perfect and not because I feel overly happy. I'm choosing to rejoice in today because it is the day You made. And I know it is good because You are good. Thank You for loving me today and every day. Thank You for giving me a reason to rejoice! Amen.

God Hears You

✧

Read 1 John 5:13-20

KEY VERSES

This is the confidence we have in approaching God: that if we ask anything according to his will, he hears us. And if we know that he hears us—whatever we ask—we know that we have what we asked of him.

1 JOHN 5:14-15 NIV

.

UNDERSTAND

- Are you confident that God hears your prayers? Why or why not?
- How can you know your prayers are in line with God's will? *Believing is will and grace that binds us together as on unit*

APPLY

From an early age, children are taught that praying is thanking God and asking Him for things that they need or want to happen. If we're not careful, we can incorrectly think of God as a heavenly vending machine that will dole out the goods if we say the right words and push the right buttons.

But prayer is *not* about pushing our agenda and hoping God will be on board with it. Prayer is approaching our loving Father with a heart that sincerely wants to be in line with His. When we pray this way, the things we ask of Him will fit into His good and perfect will for our lives and His creation as a whole. And *that's* when He hears us and we will receive what we have asked for.

What is God's will? Ask Him to show you. Seek Him in His Word. Talk to friends who are strong in their faith, and see what God is doing in their lives. He's listening. He hears you.

PRAY

Father, I am confident in my prayers to You. Give me Your wisdom to approach You with requests that You will hear and grant. I long to be in the center of Your good and perfect plan, God. Amen.

Practice Secret Blessings

Read Matthew 6:1-4

KEY VERSES

*"But when you give to the needy,
do not let your left hand know what your
right hand is doing, so that your giving may
be in secret. Then your Father, who sees
what is done in secret, will reward you."*

MATTHEW 6:3-4 NIV

UNDERSTAND

- Have you ever received a blessing in secret? How was it different than if you'd known who was behind the giving?
- Aside from God's promise of rewarding your secret generosity, why is giving in secret appealing?
- How can you meet a need in secret today?

APPLY

Pleasant surprises are one of life's greatest gifts. Whether you're on the giving or receiving end, a generous surprise that fills a need can buoy a spirit, turn a bad day into the best one, and even be a turning point in someone's life.

But God, in His wisdom, knows that when we give publicly—in a way that proclaims our goodness and generosity—it has a way of puffing up our pride. It feels good to be appreciated after all! If we're not careful, we're setting ourselves up to be praised above the One who is the Giver of all good things.

That's why He asks us to give in secret. Give anonymously. Give with a thankful heart, hopeful that the recipient directs all gratitude to the Great Provider as well. Even though others don't see you, He sees you, and that's what's important.

PRAY

Generous God, thank You for the ability to give to others—to meet real needs in Your name. Show me opportunities to give in secret, and keep my motives pure so that I'm not seeking praise or glory for myself. Everything I have is from You, Father. I am so blessed. Amen.

You Are Resilient

Read Zephaniah 3:14-20

KEY VERSES

"Do not fear, Zion; do not let your hands hang limp. The LORD your God is with you, the Mighty Warrior who saves. He will take great delight in you; in his love he will no longer rebuke you, but will rejoice over you with singing."

ZEPHANIAH 3:16–17 NIV

UNDERSTAND

- What challenge are you facing today that has your hands hanging limp?
- What makes you feel strong?
- How does it change your perspective when you realize that God, the Mighty Warrior who saves, is with you?

APPLY

Each single day brings its own challenges, but life often hurls difficult seasons at us. For days, weeks, months, or years, challenging times can leave us weary, afraid, and may even threaten to defeat us.

What are you facing today?

Take courage, for you are the daughter of the mighty Lord. Be confident in the fact that you are a resilient woman of God—not because of your own strength but because God, the King and Mighty Warrior who saves, is with you. He will not make fun of you for struggling in times of distress—He wants to love you, protect you, and fight with you through it. He takes delight in you and rejoices over you with singing! He is your Rescuer and the reason you can overcome any challenge you face.

Praise Him for past victories and stand strong in Him today.

PRAY

Defender God, thank You for saving me. I praise You for the strength You instill in me. Today I will lift my head and raise my hands in Your victory even in the midst of my struggles. I delight in You, Father. Your ways are good and perfect, so please lead me today. Amen.

God Knows Your Name

∂

Read Isaiah 43:1–13

KEY VERSE

*"Do not be afraid, for I have ransomed you.
I have called you by name; you are mine."*
ISAIAH 43:1 NLT

UNDERSTAND

- What does the fact that God calls each of us by name tell you about Him?
- How does God demonstrate to you that you are precious to Him? *with his gifts*
- Who can you encourage today by reminding them that God knows their name?

APPLY

As small children, we instinctually give names to the possessions and people dearest to us. From a name for a beloved toy or a pet to a loving nickname for a sibling or a grandparent, putting our own label on something seems to say, "I've claimed you. You are mine."

God does the same for us, His cherished children. He doesn't merely group us together and love us as a mass of humanity. No, our Father God calls us *each* by name. He promises to be with *each* of us when we are going through difficulties. He has ransomed *each* of us and claimed *each* of us as His prized possession.

Our Creator knew us before He formed us. Before our parents imagined our names, He knew us and claimed us. Listen for His voice as He whispers your name today, and know that your identity is in Him.

PRAY

God, when I read Isaiah 43, I am overwhelmed by Your kindness to me. You tell me I am precious to You and You love me. You remind me again and again that You are with me no matter what and that I have nothing to fear. Forgive me when I forget these truths. Write them on my heart so I will always find my security in You. Amen.

The Best Gift

Read Ephesians 2:1-10

KEY VERSE

For by His loving-favor you have been saved from the punishment of sin through faith. It is not by anything you have done. It is a gift of God.
EPHESIANS 2:8 NLV

UNDERSTAND

- When you understand that your salvation isn't based on how good you are or your achievements or work in God's kingdom, how does that change your perception of God?
- God made a way for your salvation long before you accepted His gift. What does that tell you about His will and plans for your life?

APPLY

Hard work is valuable. Diligence and a can-do attitude to finish a job right are admirable. Achievement and giving your best no matter what are important and can lead to personal satisfaction and rewarding results. But all these things rely on self, and if we could earn grace based on a points system, we'd compare our grace with the grace others have earned. We'd become our own saviors instead of relying on the saving work that Jesus did when He died on the cross.

God's good plan for our salvation is that He offers it freely to everyone who accepts His gift. Well before we learned such a gift was available to us, He designed and executed that perfect gift through Jesus.

Your salvation is God's good work. Praise Him today for His best gift!

PRAY

Life-giving God, I am absolutely thankful for Your gift of salvation. It's a gift that seems too good to be true, yet Your promises never fail, and I have full confidence that I am saved by Your grace. Help me to lead others to accept Your gift, Father. Give me the words and actions that show Your loving-kindness to everyone around me. Amen.

You Are Adopted by a Loving Father

Read Ephesians 1:3-14

KEY VERSE

God decided in advance to adopt us into his own family by bringing us to himself through Jesus Christ. This is what he wanted to do, and it gave him great pleasure.
EPHESIANS 1:5 NLT

UNDERSTAND

- How does knowing that God adopted His children into His family change your perception of your brothers and sisters in Christ?
- Jesus is God's only Son, but you are an adopted sister to Christ, with full privileges to share in the inheritance of God's kingdom. What does this mean to you?

APPLY

Adopting a child is a big undertaking. It's not just the time and process—often filled with paperwork and protocol and interviews and red tape—it's also a pricey endeavor, costing anywhere from a few thousand dollars to much, much more.

But for parents who have already taken a child into their heart and family, no paperwork is too lengthy. No red tape is too frustrating. No cost is too high. The child is already perfectly loved, well before signatures are on the adoption papers.

So much more is our heavenly Father's love for you. God set the adoption into motion, and your Savior and brother, Jesus, cut through the red tape and paid the ultimate price to make sure you could become His sister.

Today, thank God for making your adoption and salvation a family affair, dear one. God's grace and kindness cover you, His daughter.

PRAY

Father, I am overwhelmed when I consider the fact that You see me as worthy of being Your adopted, chosen daughter. Because of my brother, Jesus, You see me as holy and blameless. I don't deserve such favor, but I gratefully accept it. Amen.

You Are Confident in Hope

〜

Read Ephesians 1:15-23

KEY VERSE

I pray that your hearts will be flooded with light so that you can understand the confident hope he has given to those he called—his holy people who are his rich and glorious inheritance.

EPHESIANS 1:18 NLT

UNDERSTAND

Make my Steps clear

- How does knowing that God calls you His child give you confident hope?
- What does it mean that you are God's rich and glorious inheritance? *his daughter*
- Where do you need God's power to be evident in your life today?

speak

APPLY

Where light shines brightly, you can be confident in your next step. You don't fear unseen obstacles or holes to fall into. You can see your surroundings as they are and not wonder what's really out there. That kind of bright light is what Paul is praying illuminates the hearts of the believers in Ephesus—light that leads them to greater understanding, spiritual wisdom, and confident hope in today, tomorrow, and forever.

The hope we have through God's grace is not a mystical, vague feeling that everything will be okay. Our confident hope is a complete, steadfast understanding that we will be victorious through God. This certainty comes to us through the Holy Spirit who works in us.

Just as the sun rises this morning, ask God to flood your heart with His light. He will give you confident hope as you face today's challenges. You've got this, because God's got this.

PRAY

Jesus, You are the Light of the world. Shine on me today. Holy Spirit, You are my Helper. Move in my heart today. God, You are my Mighty Defender. Walk ahead of me today and be victorious over the struggles and frustrations and roadblocks that inevitably come my way. Amen.

You Can Be Content

❧

Read Philippians 4:10–20

Key Verses

I know how to live on almost nothing or with everything. I have learned the secret of living in every situation, whether it is with a full stomach or empty, with plenty or little. For I can do everything through Christ, who gives me strength.

Philippians 4:12–13 NLT

Understand

- In what areas of your life are you most content? Why?
- In what areas of your life are you most discontented? Why?

Apply

Contentment is one of those virtues that the world almost entirely dismisses. Why should anyone be content when there's always more to be had? More wealth, more power, more status, better toys, bigger houses, newer technology, latest trends. But all that striving leaves us exhausted, frustrated, and discontent in heart and mind.

So, what's the best way to practice contentment? Start with an attitude of thankfulness. When you take stock in the ways God provides for you, when you praise Him for all He's done, your heart will learn the secret to living satisfied and grateful in any situation. God will give you the strength and the untold peace that can only be found in Him.

Contentment doesn't come naturally to many of us, so start this morning by being intentional in thanking God. When you focus on His goodness, the world's shouted messages of "More, more, more!" will become nothing but background noise.

PRAY

God, I admit that I struggle with being content. My selfishness always seems to compare my situation with someone who has a little bit more. Forgive me for being ungrateful for all You provide. Teach me to be content in any situation, and if ends aren't meeting, give me the faith to trust that You will provide. Because I know You will. Amen.

God's Doing Big Things

Read Isaiah 43:14-21

KEY VERSE

*"For I am about to do something new.
See, I have already begun! Do you not see it?
I will make a pathway through the wilderness.
I will create rivers in the dry wasteland."*

ISAIAH 43:19 NLT

UNDERSTAND

- Recall a time when you know God moved in a mighty way to make something happen. How does it make you feel to know that He is ready to do something even greater?
- What is God doing in your life today?
- What's the biggest change for the better you can imagine in your life?

APPLY

We all have seasons of stagnation. There are times when we're unsatisfied with the way things are, but we are either unable or unwilling to make the adjustments necessary to change the situation. Maybe you're under an avalanche of debt. Maybe you have a relationship that is strained or breaking. Maybe you need to lose weight for the sake of your own health and your family, but the number on the scale hasn't budged in years.

Whatever situation you're thinking of, God is moving! Just like He did for the Israelites fleeing Egypt, He will make a way across the Red Sea when there seems to be no way. Here's the key: in order to get there, we must be following Him.

Are you willing to take the steps to allow God to change your situation? It may mean seeking help from experts, it may mean your time and resources. It will not be easy; it may not be quick—but God is faithful, and He is doing something new. Can you feel it?

PRAY

I'm ready for change, God. Lead me through this wilderness to Your promised land. Show me what You will have me do. Amen.

A Fresh Start

❧

Read Lamentations 3:22–33

KEY VERSES

Because of the LORD's great love we are not consumed, for his compassions never fail. They are new every morning; great is your faithfulness.
LAMENTATIONS 3:22–23 NIV

UNDERSTAND

- What comfort do you take knowing that God's compassion doesn't run out?
- Why do you think morning is a good time to seek God's forgiveness?
- Who in your life needs to receive daily mercy from you (whether they ask for it or not)?

APPLY

Yesterday is done, and you messed it up again. You snapped at your kids and husband. You told that little fib at work. Through a lens of green, you saw the neighbors' new SUV and slammed the door of your junky vehicle a little harder than necessary. You told yourself you'll never be good enough, so why even try?

Yesterday felt like a train wreck, but this morning is a new day, and your Father God is here. He's saying, "Let's start again."

The truth is that God's forgiveness is available to us any hour of the day. He is faithful to show mercy whenever we ask Him for help. But time spent with our Father in the morning will result in a clear focus, renewed hope, and a greater understanding of our worth in Christ. It sets the day into motion in the best way possible.

PRAY

Merciful Father, this morning I seek Your refreshing forgiveness. I had every intention of perfection yesterday, but I messed up again. I'm ashamed of my sin, but I'm choosing to look up to You and admit I need Your kind compassion every day. I dedicate this new day to You, God. And I will live it as Your imperfect child who is perfectly loved by You. Amen.

There's More Than This

ॐ

Read Revelation 21:1–8

KEY VERSE

"He will wipe away every tear from their eyes, and death shall be no more, neither shall there be mourning, nor crying, nor pain anymore, for the former things have passed away."

REVELATION 21:4 ESV

UNDERSTAND

- How does knowing there is something more after this life help you face today?
- What is one way you imagine heaven might be like?
- How might your relationship with God be different when you are fully present with Him in eternity?

APPLY

This old earth is broken and full of sadness. Stresses pile up and frustrations mount. Loss leaves us reeling, and pain is inevitable. In seasons when it feels like Murphy's Law reigns, we begin to wonder if the hurting will ever stop.

Revelation 21:4 is an encouraging Bible promise that we can cling to during the darkest times. Eternity for Christians includes a new heaven, a new earth, and a new reality that we simply cannot comprehend. No tears. No death or mourning or crying or pain.

Even better—God will make His home with us. He will dwell among us, closer than a next-door neighbor. We will have unbridled access to Him and all His goodness and mercy and love and abundance.

No one can say for certain what heaven will be like, but imagine what amazing things lie in store. And praise God for them.

PRAY

Heavenly Father, I am so thankful for the confidence I have in an eternity with You. I can't fathom the wonders that Your creative hand has in store for the new heaven and the new earth, and I can't wait to see Your masterful work! I long for that renewal personally too. Make me new today; change me to be more like You. Amen.

New Clothes

Read Colossians 3:1–14

KEY VERSE

Therefore, as God's chosen people, holy and dearly loved, clothe yourselves with compassion, kindness, humility, gentleness, and patience.
COLOSSIANS 3:12 NIV

UNDERSTAND

- When you experience God's compassion, how does that influence the compassion you show to others?
- Of the list of compassion, kindness, humility, gentleness, and patience, which is the easiest for you to demonstrate?
- Which is the most challenging for you to demonstrate?

APPLY

How much time do you take to choose an outfit each day? Do you lay it out the night before, complete with specific accessories? Or do you tug on whatever smells cleanest from the hamper?

Just as our physical clothes say something

about who we are, Paul is urging his readers in <u>Colossians 3</u> to clothe themselves with the attributes of Christ Jesus: compassion, kindness, humility, gentleness, and patience. Why does Paul use the clothing analogy? Because clothing is something that we must intentionally put on; we come out of the womb without wearing a stitch!

Which articles of Jesus' clothing does today call for? All these things layer well and help prepare you for any climate. Best of all, when you dress yourself in these clothes, you're looking even more like the love of God.

Today, take stock in the ways that God shows you <u>compassion</u>, <u>kindness</u>, <u>gentleness</u>, and <u>patience</u>. Ask Him for opportunities to show these to others as well.

PRAY

God, I want to be more like You. You shower me with compassion and kindness. But my own selfishness gets in the way of being like You—I am proud and impatient with others. Help me to realize how much I have been forgiven, how much You love me, so that I can show this same love to others. Amen.

Love Difficult People

Read Luke 6:27–35

KEY VERSES

"I say to you who hear Me, love those who work against you. Do good to those who hate you. Respect and give thanks for those who try to bring bad to you. Pray for those who make it very hard for you."

LUKE 6:27–28 NLV

UNDERSTAND

- Who is the most difficult person in your life, and what makes them such a challenge?
- How, practically, can you do something good and show respect for this person today?
- How could your perspective change if you make it a priority to pray for this person?

APPLY

Most of us are conflict-avoiders. Apart from those rare few who are wired to enjoy a good combative exchange, we intentionally structure our lives to be harmonious in whatever ways we can.

But there's always that person who is just so difficult. Maybe it's a coworker who seems to sabotage your efforts. Maybe it's an in-law who has never warmed to your presence in the family. Maybe it's someone who struggles socially, and it comes across as disrespect, creating awkward situations. Maybe it's simply someone who doesn't like you, and they make no qualms about it.

Jesus says love them anyway. Do good to them. Respect them and pray for them. This might be one of Jesus' most challenging commands, yet He demonstrated it over and over in His ministry on earth. With His help, you can do it.

PRAY

This is a hard one, God. I receive no respect, so everything inside me wants to disrespect in return. And love them? Do good to them? I can't do this on my own, Father. Inhabit this relationship. Give me Your eyes to see them the way You see them. That's the only way I will be able to love. Amen.

Three Things for Today
∽

Read 1 Thessalonians 5:12–22

Key Verses

Always be joyful. Never stop praying. Be thankful in all circumstances, for this is God's will for you who belong to Christ Jesus.
1 Thessalonians 5:16–18 NLT

Understand

- How would your life be different if you were *always* joyful?
- Could you take your thoughts and self-talk and turn them into conversations with God?
- Do you think it's possible to be thankful in all circumstances? Why or why not?

Apply

How often should we be joyful? *Always*—the apostle Paul doesn't mince words in his letter to the church in Thessalonica. And when can we stop praying? *Never*—again, he makes the expectation clear. He concludes this three-part to-do list just as strong: Be thankful—for everything and in every situation.

If it feels like adding these three directives to your stressful daily life is impossible, consider this: if we work toward the attitudes of joy and thankfulness, the frustrations and stresses of the day won't be so monumental. And when we continually talk to God, we have an outlet for the good, the bad, and the ugly of our days. These three things are simple ways to stay connected to the true Source of all goodness!

Today, be joyful, never stop praying, and be thankful, and see how God transforms your overall outlook!

PRAY

Father, I admit that sometimes my joy gets buried deep under the daily stresses of life. Restore to me my joy in You. Today I will pray to You with every breath I take. And I will find new joy in You in every circumstance—not just the happy ones but in all circumstances. Thank You for loving me. Thank You for choosing me. Thank You for leading me in Your goodness. Amen.

You Don't Have to Understand Everything

~

Read Isaiah 55:6–13

KEY VERSES

"For My thoughts are not your thoughts, and My ways are not your ways," says the Lord. "For as the heavens are higher than the earth, so are My ways higher than your ways, and My thoughts than your thoughts."

ISAIAH 55:8–9 NLV

UNDERSTAND

- How do you feel when you don't understand something? *Lost*
- How does it change when you don't understand, but you do trust the person who is in control of the situation? *Because Gods in cola*
- Can you trust God even when you don't understand what He's thinking or doing? Why or why not?

APPLY

If we can't be in control, it at least helps when we understand why something is happening.

But God doesn't promise us understanding. In fact, there are some things about God we simply *cannot* grasp this side of heaven.

God says in scripture that His ways are "far beyond anything you could imagine" (Isaiah 55:8 NLT). That doesn't mean that He won't give us insight into what He's doing, but the fact remains that sometimes His plans may seem confusing and downright undecipherable to our human minds.

Rather than letting this scripture frustrate you, take comfort and encouragement in knowing that you don't have to understand everything. You don't have to have everything under control and figured out! God's ways are the *best* ways, and He will never leave you. He is working a perfect plan in you and around you.

PRAY

Lord God, sometimes Your ways are a complete mystery to me. I don't understand what You're doing, and I realize—yet again— that I'm not in control. But the truth is, I am thankful Your ways and plans are better, more holy, and absolutely perfect. So even when I don't understand, lead on. Amen.

You Can Reach Your Goals

Read Isaiah 40:22–31

KEY VERSES

He gives strength to the weary and increases the power of the weak. Even youths grow tired and weary, and young men stumble and fall; but those who hope in the LORD will renew their strength. They will soar on wings like eagles; they will run and not grow weary, they will walk and not be faint.

ISAIAH 40:29–31 NIV

UNDERSTAND

- What have you accomplished only because of God's strength?
- In what area of your life do you need to ask God for strength and stamina?

APPLY

You may know in your head and heart there's nothing that God Himself cannot do, but do you realize that He wants to renew your strength so *you* can do great things as well?

What big, audacious dreams do you have?

Maybe the burdens of life have buried these goals in your heart, but with God by your side, you can bring them back to life today! Put your hope in the Lord, ask Him to guide your plans, and He will renew your desire.

Working toward a dream isn't easy, but it is achievable. When you start to see results, momentum toward the goal—that's when you will feel as though you are soaring on eagles' wings. With God's help, you will press on and not get tired.

He's here, cheering you on right now. Do you hear that encouraging voice full of love?

PRAY

God, I have so many dreams and goals, but sometimes I don't know where to begin. Show me what You want for me, and set me on the path toward those goals. Put the drive and tenacity in my heart to make them happen. I give You all the glory for any success I will have. Amen.

Guilt-Free

∽

Read Psalm 103:8-18

KEY VERSES

For as high as the heavens are above the earth, so great is his love for those who fear him; as far as the east is from the west, so far has he removed our transgressions from us.
PSALM 103:11-12 NIV

UNDERSTAND

- What is your favorite word picture for the enormity of God's love?
- Why is it essential that we serve a God of extremes and absolutes?
- What role should guilt play in our lives as Christians?

APPLY

Aren't you thankful that our God is a God of extremes? His love for His children knows no bounds—it reaches to the heavens (Psalm 103:11) and is everlasting (v. 17). His forgiveness is absolute, and He removes our sins "as far as the east is from the west" (v. 12 NIV).

If we believe these truths, then why do we still struggle with guilt?

One reason is that the prince of this world, Satan, is constantly reminding us of our past. Fleeting thoughts and temptations may trigger memories of who we used to be before we knew Christ. Strongholds of sin that we still struggle with rear their ugly heads. And suddenly we feel unworthy, unloved, and unfit to be a child of the King.

But our extreme God can free us of guilty feelings—right now! Lay your struggles before the throne, and allow His peace to wash over you.

PRAY

Father God, I already know I am forgiven, and I believe it when scripture says that You have removed my sins as far as the east is from the west. But I still feel guilt over the past, and I can't seem to shake it. Please take my guilt as far away as my sins. Amen.

Shame-Free

❧

Read Isaiah 50:4-9

KEY VERSE

Because the Sovereign LORD helps me, I will not be disgraced. Therefore have I set my face like flint, and I know I will not be put to shame.
ISAIAH 50:7 NIV

UNDERSTAND

- If you struggle with shame, is it because of your own inner thoughts? Or are you ashamed because of how others perceive you?
- Do you think God is ashamed of you? Why or why not?
- What is the remedy for shame?

APPLY

If we're living out God's good plan for our lives, we will sometimes make decisions and take stands that go against the popular opinion of the world. When these times come, it can be downright frightening to open our inner selves to be ridiculed, mocked, and even shamed.

But God is there, and He will help you. Seek wisdom in His Word, talk to believing friends and family, ask for their support, and follow the guidance of the Holy Spirit.

What do you need to take a stand for today? If you've been avoiding it, it's never too late to change course and show God's light and kindness and love in any situation. Scripture tells us that God has not given us a spirit of fear. Rather, He's given us a powerful, loving spirit and a sound mind that can hold fast to His promises (see 2 Timothy 1:7).

PRAY

Father, I admit that sometimes I don't act because I fear how it will be perceived by others. Forgive me for not trusting that You will keep me from being disgraced. When all is said and done, I know what You think of me is all that matters, but I want to be liked, respected, and accepted by everyone. Show me Your will in all things. Amen.

How You'll Be Remembered

❧

Read 2 Timothy 1:3–11

KEY VERSE

*I remember your genuine faith, for you share
the faith that first filled your grandmother
Lois and your mother, Eunice. And I know
that same faith continues strong in you.*
2 TIMOTHY 1:5 NLT

UNDERSTAND

- Who has been instrumental in passing their faith to you?
- Who are you passing your faith to?
- Someday when people are remembering your legacy on earth, what is the first thing you hope they would say about you?

APPLY

The apostle Paul's young protégé, Timothy, was blessed with a heritage of faith, passed down through multiple generations. Paul writes of Timothy's grandmother and mother as being instrumental in building a strong foundation for his life of service to God.

Whether your family tree is made up of branches strong in faith or you are the first offshoot growing in the Lord, your faith legacy is an important part of your story.

This morning, think about the people who had the most influence in your decision to come to Christ and who have helped you grow. Spend time thanking God for their love and care for you. And then think about who you are passing your faith to. One of the beautiful things about God's family tree is that it isn't constrained by bloodlines. You can be a spiritual grandmother, mother, or sister to *anyone*. Pray and ask God to show you who you can pour His love into today.

PRAY

Father, thank You for the heritage of faith in my life. I am humbled when I think about the people who loved me so much that they led me to Your Son. I want to pass on the legacy of Your goodness and salvation to the next generation. Show me who. Show me how. Give me Your heart. Amen.

You Are Not Alone

❧

Read Psalm 23

KEY VERSE

Yes, even if I walk through the valley of the shadow of death, I will not be afraid of anything, because You are with me.

PSALM 23:4 NLV

UNDERSTAND

- Do you believe that, with the Lord as your Shepherd, you have everything you need? Why or why not?
- When do you feel God's presence most near?
- Which word pictures in Psalm 23 are most comforting to you? Why?

APPLY

From an early age, we're taught to be self-reliant. To work hard and figure it out and provide for ourselves and our loved ones. Plans and hard work are commendable, and scripture encourages us to pursue both (see Proverbs 21:5), but Psalm 23 shows us the picture of God as our Shepherd providing everything we need as His sheep.

A shepherd is ever-present with his flock, keeping watch over them, leading them to water for refreshment and green grass for nourishment. He keeps his sheep out of danger and walks with them along treacherous paths. He ensures that his sheep are *never alone*.

If you feel alone today, take solace in Psalm 23. The truth is when we *feel* alone, we aren't *actually* alone. Grasp ahold of God's promise that He is with you, and you will have everything you need.

PRAY

God, I feel alone. But my feelings often can't be trusted. My head and heart know that You are here. You are my vigilant Shepherd, and I am Your beloved lamb. Guide me through the dark valleys of life. And please use Your staff to keep me on the path with You. I do not want to stray from Your loving presence. Amen.

Pray for Our Leaders

Read 1 Timothy 2:1-15

KEY VERSES

I urge, then, first of all, that petitions, prayers, intercession and thanksgiving be made for all people—for kings and all those in authority, that we may live peaceful and quiet lives in all godliness and holiness.

1 TIMOTHY 2:1–2 NIV

UNDERSTAND

- Why do you think Paul urges Timothy to pray for governmental leaders?
- Is it possible to pray for leaders with whom you disagree? Why or why not?
- What leader or current situation can you pray for today?

APPLY

No matter which political party you declare in a primary election, regardless of your leaning to the left or to the right, and even if you didn't vote for whoever is currently in office, as Christians, we must pray for our leaders—local, state, and national alike.

In our current political environment, this is sometimes a tough pill to swallow. Odds are there's *someone* in authority whose policies or beliefs we strongly disagree with. But praying for a leader isn't entirely about them. It's more about a heart transformation for us.

You see, when we're sincerely interceding for others, they become less of a talking head from a news clip and more of a real person, made in the image of God. We consider the challenging position they are in, and with God's help, we may start to see them with the eyes of Jesus.

PRAY

Father, my soul longs for peaceful unity, but politically I feel none. Give me Your heart for the leaders and people in authority of my town, my state, and my nation. Press upon my spirit a name or two that You want me to specifically pray for. Give them pure hearts to lead well and do what is right in Your eyes. Amen.

Your Ransom Is Paid

Read 1 Peter 1:13–19

KEY VERSES

For you know that God paid a ransom to save you from the empty life you inherited from your ancestors. And it was not paid with mere gold or silver, which lose their value. It was the precious blood of Christ, the sinless, spotless Lamb of God.

1 PETER 1:18–19 NLT

UNDERSTAND

- Are there limits to what you would give to pay a ransom for someone you love? Why or why not?
- What does the ransom that God paid for your new life say about the value He places on you?

APPLY

You've probably never thought of your salvation in terms of a Liam Neeson film from the "Taken" franchise, but the apostle Peter's ransom analogy gives us a new way to think about our salvation.

Satan laid claim to humankind way back in

the Garden of Eden when Adam and Eve ate the forbidden fruit. And each of us has followed in their footsteps, giving in to our own selfish desires and sinning. But even before we thought of God, He thought of us and put up the <u>priceless</u> <u>treasure</u> of <u>His Son's life for ours.</u>

Can you imagine the delight Satan must've taken in such a trade? Our worthless souls for the sinless Jesus! But the Father knew that was not the end. Final victory was His—and ours—on the third day when Jesus came back to life!

PRAY

Jesus, when I think of how Your precious blood paid the ransom for my life, I am humbled to the point of tears. I don't deserve such generosity, such love, such grace. But You willingly went to the cross to finish the nasty business of Satan's claim on my soul. My heart is Yours. My soul is Yours. Make me more like You. Amen.

How Much God Loves the World

❧

Read John 3:16-21

KEY VERSE

"For this is how God loved the world: He gave his one and only Son, so that everyone who believes in him will not perish but have eternal life."
JOHN 3:16 NLT

UNDERSTAND

- What does the John 3:16 scripture reveal about the love of God?
- What do God's actions reveal about what He thinks of us?

APPLY

God could've created the world, set it spinning on its axis, and walked away. He could've fashioned humans from dust, and as soon as we messed up our relationship with Him, He could've left us to our own devices—moved on to create something else that maybe wouldn't betray Him. But He didn't. He loves us too much to leave us in our own filth.

He loves the world so much that He gave up the One most precious to Him: His Son. It defies logic, but it's absolutely true. God willingly handed Jesus over to be sacrificed for the sin of the world. Not just your sins. Not just the sins of the people who have already accepted His grace. Jesus died for the sins of the *whole history of the world*.

Love is a powerful force. The love of God is an unstoppable force. Today, live in that all-encompassing love God has for you.

PRAY

Merciful, loving Father, Your love is rooted in the most giving, unselfish act in all of history. As difficult as it was for Jesus to lay down His own life, how much harder must it have been for You to give up Your beloved Son to be a human and spiritual sacrifice. Thank You for loving the world so much that You made a way when there was no other way. Amen.

You Can Trust Him

⁓

Read Proverbs 3:1-12

KEY VERSES

Trust in the LORD with all your heart; do not depend on your own understanding. Seek his will in all you do, and he will show you which path to take.

PROVERBS 3:5-6 NLT

UNDERSTAND

- In what areas of your life is it easy to trust God? *Health*
- In what areas of your life is it difficult to trust God?
- When have you trusted God and clearly seen the path He wanted you to take?

APPLY

What decision are you facing currently? Our lives are made up of big decisions and small decisions—some require a choice right now and some must be thought about, debated, and weighed.

Your loving Father can and wants to give

you wisdom in every decision. No choice is too trivial, no problem is too big, no challenge is too insurmountable for Him to guide you through it.

Today, whether you're facing a big decision or not, pray and ask the Holy Spirit to come alive in your heart. Seek out His truth in scripture, and ask Him to make His will obvious to you. Then talk to mature Christian friends whom you trust. The Lord is faithful to show you which path is His, and you can step confidently forward as you follow Him.

Pray

Lord God, I admit there are times I'd rather trust my gut than trust You. When I'm in danger of relying on my own wits to make a decision, remind me that Your will is what I want to follow. Make the pathway ahead obvious and cleared of obstacles so that I will walk confidently ahead. Be the King of my heart today and every day, Father. Amen.

Take Delight in the Lord

※

Read Psalm 37:1–9

KEY VERSE

*Take delight in the LORD, and he will
give you the desires of your heart.*
PSALM 37:4 NIV

UNDERSTAND

- What does taking delight in the Lord mean
  to you? *Calling to Shine when thing*
  where dark to light they
- In what ways do you imagine the Lord
  delights in you? *understanding his will of*
  to gether ness
- Is Psalm 37:4 saying that God will give us
  anything we ask for? Why or why not?
  to those that have kept near to
  his side in all thing good or bad

APPLY

Children are experts in delight. Watch a one-
year-old gleefully play with the box her birthday
present came wrapped in, and you are witness-
ing true joy. We can learn much from her today.

Our outlook determines how we interact
with the world around us. When we're thankful
for and take joy in simple pleasures, disappointments and frustrations become minor bumps in

the day rather than catastrophes that derail us. When we count our blessings instead of focusing on what we don't have, we realize how well God provides for us. When we delight in the Lord and praise Him for His goodness and His perfect plan for us, we live safely in the center of His will—the very best place to be.

How is God delighting you today? Spend time this morning looking for ways to be joyful. Whether He's doing big things in your life right now or you simply reflect on His unending faithfulness, live each day as an expert in delight.

PRAY

Lord, You fill me with such joy. Today
my heart is singing as I delight in You.
You are a good, good Father who gives me
care, compassion, and kindness every day.
Because of You, I have everything I need.
Let my heart draw close to Yours, Father.
I praise You because of who You are. Amen.

1 | 2

God's Faithfulness Has No End

Read Deuteronomy 7:6–9

Key Verse

Know therefore that the Lord your God is God; he is the faithful God, keeping his covenant of love to a thousand generations of those who love him and keep his commandments.

Deuteronomy 7:9 NIV

Understand

- How do you know you can trust God to keep His word?
- When has God been faithful to you despite your own unfaithfulness?

Apply

We humans are a fickle bunch. We go from one fad diet to the next. Today's stunning interior design is tomorrow's cheesy, dated look. From today's bestselling author to tomorrow's newest big celebrity, our attention spans grow shorter by the minute.

Thank goodness our steady God doesn't

follow whims or popular thought. When we have exhausted ourselves by trying to keep up with current trends and schools of thought, the Lord is steadfast in all things, not the least of which is that He will faithfully keep His promises to His children.

Maybe what you really need today is mental rest from chasing after the newest thing. Your loving Father provides that in His faithfulness. You don't need to wonder what He's thinking or what He's doing. He will not suddenly change His expectations or stop caring about you and move on to someone else. You have His love, and you have it forever.

PRAY

Father God, I praise You because of Your faithfulness. You are my Rock and my strong fortress that cannot be moved. I don't have to fretfully wonder what You're doing in my life because I trust You fully. Infuse my spirit with steadfastness in my relationships. I want to shine Your light of faithfulness to others in everyday life. Amen.

Seeking God's Word

Read Psalm 119:1-16

KEY VERSES

How can a young person stay on the path of purity? By living according to your word. I seek you with all my heart; do not let me stray from your commands. I have hidden your word in my heart that I might not sin against you.

PSALM 119:9–11 NIV

UNDERSTAND

- How does spending time in God's Word add to your life?
- What verses have you hidden in your heart through memorization?
- How has God's Word helped you "stay on the path of purity" (v. 9)?

APPLY

There are some items that have a knack for getting misplaced. Phones, glasses, car keys, remotes—these things are all essential, so when one is lost, we take the time and effort to seek the missing item until it's found, sometimes upending a house in order to find it!

Once you experience the power of God's Word, it becomes an essential part of your life. And when life gets busy and you're not spending time in the Bible, you feel that missing piece. Seeking His wisdom with your whole heart by opening scripture is one of the best ways to stay in tune with God's heart. When we study scripture, we're allowing the Holy Spirit to awaken and speak to us, encourage us, and convict us of areas in our lives where we need to change.

Keep seeking God's Word, and you will find your loving Father was in front of you all along!

PRAY

Almighty Lord, I am grateful for Your Word. Let Your scripture take root in my heart and soul. Help me to commit more and more of Your wisdom to memory, and let it come to mind when I need it and when I can encourage someone else. Amen.

Understanding Our Freedom

Read 2 Corinthians 3:7-18

KEY VERSES

For the Lord is the Spirit, and wherever the Spirit of the Lord is, there is freedom. So all of us who have had that <u>veil removed</u> can see and reflect the glory of the Lord. And the Lord—who is the Spirit—makes us more and more like him as we are changed into his glorious image.

2 CORINTHIANS 3:17–18 NLT

UNDERSTAND

- How does your life reflect the glory of the Lord?
- In what ways is the Spirit making you more like God?

APPLY

To really understand the freedom we have in Christ, we first must understand just how restrictive the old covenant was. Open your Bible to books like <u>Leviticus</u>, and you'll see lists of <u>ceremonial, sacrificial, and moral laws.</u> In order to be right with God, His people had to follow *each of* these laws. Break just one, and they were out of God's good favor. Living under the law was oppressive and exhausting, but the faithful also understood the effort was worth it—a blameless life meant fellowship with God—intimate friendship like Moses experienced on the mountain (see 2 Corinthians 3:13).

Under the new covenant of Christ, Jesus came to earth to satisfy all these laws and be the ultimate sacrifice for the sins of the world. No longer do we need to work to earn the Father's approval and to be His friend. All we must do is accept the free gift of grace that He offers. We don't have to climb a mountain to reflect the glory of God. We can experience His full life here, now, today!

PRAY

God, because of Jesus and the gift of Your Spirit, I know I live in freedom. Teach me how to live fully free and more like You each day. Amen.

and Everyday

Stillness Before God

❧

Read Psalm 46

KEY VERSE

*"Be still, and know that I am God! I will
be honored by every nation. I will be
honored throughout the world."*

PSALM 46:10 NLT

UNDERSTAND

- Is being still before God easy for you? Why
  or why not?
- What's one positive thing you think would
  come out of meditative stillness?

APPLY

When life is particularly chaotic, our minds and
hearts tend to shift into chaos mode as well. If
you're a natural worrier, your fret level may reach
code red. Anxiety may shoot through the roof.
You may go into defense mode and put up walls
between yourself and the people around you.
You may even try to strongarm the situation and
fix it by sheer force of will.

But all these responses mean you've forgotten that God is in control. The fact is, nothing

can happen in your life that surprises God. He knows what tomorrow will bring. He knows what today has in store. He knows your path in the next hour and even the next minute. And it's all in His capable hands.

Today, stop. Be still and take refuge in the fact that He is God and you are not. He is always ready to help in times of trouble (Psalm 46:1). He is here among us and He is our fortress (v. 7).

PRAY

God, quiet my brain. I am here with You right now in body, mind, and spirit. You are God. You are good. You are holy. You are perfect. You are my Rescuer, my Redeemer, my Shepherd, my Friend. I praise You for who You are. I praise You for all You do and all You have yet to do in the world and in my life. Amen.

Live Every Day in Awe

❧

Read Psalm 33:1–15

KEY VERSE

Let all the earth fear the LORD; let all the
inhabitants of the world stand in awe of him!
PSALM 33:8 ESV

UNDERSTAND

- When was the last time you were awestruck
  by God? **when he give me hear**,
- Why is God worthy of our awe?
- Do you think it's possible to increase your
  awe of God in your everyday life? Why or
  why not?

APPLY

If you ever doubt the power of words, remember this: Our Creator God spoke the world into
being (Psalm 33:9). "Let there be light," He said
in Genesis 1:3, and light appeared. From His
infinite mind and artistic sensibility, He formed
each mountain and star, each creature with its
unique look and role in His plan. And then He
sculpted us, the most beloved of His creation,

intricate and beautiful living beings made in His own image.

He gave us free will and hearts geared toward relationship—with Him and with other humans. And He loved us with a love so great that He would sacrifice everything to allow us to be with Him after we messed up our perfect relationship with Him.

The whole earth is filled with awe-inspiring reminders of God's majesty. Today, pray and ask God to open your eyes to see the reminders as they truly are and stand in awe of Him.

PRAY

My Creator and King, show me the wonder of Your creation. In the life-giving nourishment of rainfall, in the majesty of a sunset, in the twinkling of points of light in the heavens, I am amazed. You provide everything I need, and what's more is You have made all things beautiful as well. Thank You, God. Amen.

Waiting Expectantly

Read Psalm 27

KEY VERSE

Wait patiently for the LORD. Be brave and courageous. Yes, wait patiently for the LORD.
PSALM 27:14 NLT

UNDERSTAND

- What are the things in life you consider worth waiting for? *self, family*
- Why is waiting so hard? *i got used to it*
- Is it possible to wait without worrying? Why or why not?

No time to worry God got it he tell me

APPLY

God's timing is perfect. Even when we believe this fact wholeheartedly, waiting for Him to act at the right time is difficult. Scripture encourages us again and again to wait patiently on our Father, who knows everything and is in complete control, and to pray earnestly while waiting. Psalm 27:14 goes further by giving us an action step while we wait: be brave and courageous.

What does this mean on a practical level?

It means during seasons of waiting, we can live every day having full confidence knowing that God *will* act. We can anticipate that He will do something in a delightfully surprising and altogether perfect way. With courage, we can stand tall and say to ourselves and others, "God's got this handled."

What are you waiting on today? Keep praying, asking for God to act in that situation, and also ask for a dose of bravery to lift your spirit. He will fill you with courage and the eager anticipation of the answer to your prayer.

PRAY

I don't like to wait, God. Even when I trust in Your perfect timing, I struggle. I worry. I fret. I want to take control of the situation and force my will. Give me patience. But today I'm also asking for courage. Make me brave to live in the confidence that You have this well under control and that You're lining up all the details for Your will to be done in my life. Amen.

Praise the Lord in the Morning and Evening

Read Psalm 92

KEY VERSES

It is good to praise the Lord and make music to your name, O Most High, proclaiming your love in the morning and your faithfulness at night.

PSALM 92:1–2 NIV

UNDERSTAND

- What do you do in the morning to intentionally set the tone for your day?
- Why do you think the psalm writer suggests that we proclaim God's love in the morning?
- . . .and His faithfulness at night?

APPLY

For even the most spontaneous, schedule-adverse person, everyone has certain life rhythms. We live by the rising and setting of the sun; we have bookends to each day. This beginning and end is the perfect time to reset our hearts to align with God.

Psalm 92 tells us that it's good to praise the Lord in the morning and celebrate His love. Why? Because throughout the day the world will beat us down with messages that we are unworthy, unqualified, unloved. And starting out the day rooted in the unending love of God will keep us standing strong.

He then goes on to tell us to praise God at night and focus on His faithfulness. Why? Because God showed up throughout the day—in big ways and in small. He kept us going during moments of stress and anxiety, and He kept His promises. Reminding ourselves of His faithfulness helps us remember His unending goodness the next time we're struggling.

Praise Him this morning. Live in His love and faithfulness.

PRAY

God of love, thank You for lavishing Your care and devotion on me. I am made whole in Your love this morning. When I'm feeling unloved, unworthy, and forgotten today, wrap Your arms around me and remind me that I am Yours. Amen.

Live in Hope

≈

Read Psalm 147

KEY VERSE

The LORD's delight is in those who fear him,
those who put their hope in his unfailing love.
PSALM 147:11 NLT

UNDERSTAND

- Why do you think God delights when we put our hope in His love?
- Do you have hope today? Why or why not?
- What situation in your life needs an infusion of hope today?

APPLY

Hope is a wonderful, ever-present thing for Christians. When life is good and everything feels harmonious, when the birds sing and the sun shines, we are filled with hope. And when life is in turmoil and everything feels discordant, when the birds screech, the wind howls, and everything feels wrong, still we hope.

Why? Because God has never failed us yet,

and He won't start failing us now. God's love is there, holding us up. God's plan continues even when we don't see it or understand it. God's Spirit sustains us as we hold on to hope.

And God delights in our hope. Celebrate hope on the days it comes easy, and ask Him to supply you with an extra dose of hope on the days it comes harder. Praise God for the hope you have in His promises, in His love, and in His care for you. Cling to hope when life feels impossible, but don't give up. Hold on, child. The Father is coming.

PRAY

Father, thank You for Your sustaining hope. I know I can trust You in all things, and that fact is a great source of comfort to me. I know difficult times will come, but I also know that Your love never fails. Help me to shine Your love and Your light of hope to people around me who may feel hopeless. You have not forgotten them. Amen.

Keep Going

Read Galatians 6:1–10

KEY VERSE

Do not let yourselves get tired of doing good. If we do not give up, we will get what is coming to us at the right time.
GALATIANS 6:9 NLV

UNDERSTAND

- How do you persevere when you feel as though your efforts for God's kingdom are in vain?
- How can you know you're spending time on the things God wants you to be doing for Him?
- How can you rest without stopping?

APPLY

Oftentimes doing good work in the Lord's name is its own reward. Although we aren't saved by our good deeds, when we're demonstrating God's love to others through our efforts, we're helping to further His plan on earth. What could be better?

But other times and in some seasons of life, doing good work may feel like a burden. We may be overextended or putting unrealistic expectations on ourselves and others. The work and our attitude about the work may even be straining relationships with family and friends. Even while doing God's work, it's possible to feel far from Him.

Still, the apostle Paul says, don't give up doing good.

If you're feeling tired of doing good, look at the big picture. Ask God to renew your passion for His work and to show you what He wants you to do. Pause to rest when necessary—not disengaging entirely but allowing yourself to recharge. God will reward your faithfulness!

PRAY

God, when life gets crazy, I start to develop a bad attitude about the good things You have given me to do. Renew in me a passion for Your work. Give me eyes to see how my efforts play a part in Your plan. And encourage me in my work so I can stay excited and vitalized to do it. Amen.

Wisdom and Kindness

~

Read Proverbs 31:10–31

KEY VERSE

*She opens her mouth with wisdom, and the
teaching of kindness is on her tongue.*
PROVERBS 31:26 ESV

UNDERSTAND

- Who do you know who best embodies the
  attributes of the Proverbs 31 woman?
- When you open your mouth, are wisdom
  and kindness the first things that come out?
  If not, what usually comes out?
- What situations and relationships can you
  infuse with kindness today?

APPLY

In times of high stress and high emotions, we
may be surprised at what comes barreling out
of our mouths. We often react too quickly with
knee-jerk responses that can be thoughtless at
best and devastating at worst.

But the truth is, we have a choice in the
words we say. As difficult as it is to train our

minds and mouths, we can, like the Proverbs 31 woman, open our mouths with wisdom and demonstrate kindness with our words and actions.

Such training requires filling our minds and hearts with the wisdom that only comes from God's Word. You're doing that when you spend time in the Bible every day. Remember His promises, His kindness toward you (even when you don't deserve it), and His unending forgiveness. Then ask the Holy Spirit to guard your mouth and give you the wise, kind reaction in any scenario. Allow God's love to shine through you in any situation!

Pray

God, help me to follow Your example and the example of the Proverbs 31 woman in kindness. Give me the wisdom to understand the difference between kindness and niceness. When the world is fake, make me genuine in my interactions. You are so faithful in Your kindness toward me, and I want to reflect the same to others. Amen.

God Hears and Listens

❧

Read Psalm 66

KEY VERSES

But truly God has listened; he has attended to the voice of my prayer. Blessed be God, because he has not rejected my prayer or removed his steadfast love from me!
PSALM 66:19–20 ESV

UNDERSTAND

- What is the difference between hearing and listening?
- Scripture tells us that God both hears and listens to our prayers. Why are both important?

APPLY

Moms of young children are expert listeners. A child may talk a mile a minute about a thousand things that seem to have no common thread, but a mommy understands the precious heart behind the words. She can truly listen to the little voice.

God accepts the prayers of His children in

an even more intimate way. He hears our voice. He listens and understands our feelings and motivations behind the words. And because He created us, He knows our true hearts for the prayers we pray. As imperfect and inarticulate as we often are when speaking to our Father, He welcomes our prayers and showers us in His love.

God is speaking into our lives as well. Do we hear? We must quiet the other voices and noisemakers in our lives and really listen. After speaking to God, sit in silence and ask Him to speak. The Holy Spirit will help you hear, listen, and understand the Father's voice. When you and God are both attending to each other's voice, there's no prayer more powerful!

PRAY

Father, thank You for hearing and listening to my voice when I call to You in prayer. When You listen, I feel loved, accepted, and understood. Today I am listening for You. Speak, Lord, and I will hear and understand. Amen.

Speak Gently

Read Proverbs 15

KEY VERSE

A gentle answer turns away wrath,
but a harsh word stirs up anger.
PROVERBS 15:1 NIV

UNDERSTAND

- In your experience, how has a gentle response diffused a tense situation?
- In what situations or relationships are you more likely to respond with a harsh word?
- Do you think you'd ever regret using gentleness in an exchange?

APPLY

Words are powerful. Cliché? Yes, but that doesn't make it any less true.

Thoughtless words can unintentionally wreck someone's day. Careless words can lead to confusion and misunderstanding. Intentionally hurtful words can create lasting damage. And words used as weapons to slash at others can take a tense exchange and escalate it to a full-on angry battle.

But thoughtful, gentle words have the opposite effect and can be just as mighty. Words spoken in kindness can *make* someone's day. Encouraging words can start to rebuild a battered self-image. Loving words can mend bridges and tear down walls of resentment. A gentle response can lead to peace.

Today and every day, choose your words carefully. Thoughtfully consider the way you speak to your family, friends, frenemies, coworkers, and even how you speak to yourself. Ask God to fill your heart, mind, and tongue with wisdom to speak gentleness.

PRAY

God, I need help controlling the words that come out of my mouth. You know the people and the situations that light me up and make me see red. But I have a choice in my reactions and responses. I want to choose gentleness. I want to bring Your peace into every situation. Show me how, because I can't do it by myself. Amen.

What to Wear

∽

Read 1 Corinthians 6:12–20

KEY VERSE

"I have the right to do anything," you say—
but not everything is beneficial. "I have
the right to do anything"—but I will
not be mastered by anything.
1 CORINTHIANS 6:12 NIV

UNDERSTAND

- How do you make decisions about specific topics—like what to wear—that aren't spelled out precisely in scripture?
- How can you honor God in your wardrobe choices?
- What do you think Paul means when he says he won't be "mastered by anything"?

APPLY

If you ever doubt the freedom we have as Christian women, you need look no further than the clothing requirements put on women in many world religions—from specific head coverings and styles of clothes and the full, head-to-toe burka worn by some Muslim women.

Scripture encourages us to dress modestly, in decent and appropriate clothing that won't draw attention to ourselves (see 1 Timothy 2:9). But past those general guidelines, we are free to dress in ways that reflect our own preference and style!

How is your wardrobe communicating your heart to others? What factors influence the clothes you choose to purchase and wear? Clothing is, of course, a practical, physical matter, but for the Christian, it's also a heart matter. Don't fall for the world's lie that true, empowered femininity means dressing immodestly. Honor God and His creation (you!) by what you wear.

PRAY

Jesus, I'm so thankful that Your work on the cross allows me to live in freedom. I'm not shackled by the requirements of the Old Testament law or any other religion's regulation, and I'm so grateful for that. Give me the wisdom to live wisely in my freedom—to live in a thoughtful, intentional way that honors You. Amen.

Good in Exchange for Evil

❧

Read 1 Peter 3:8–22

KEY VERSES

*Finally, all of you, be like-minded,
be sympathetic, love one another,
be compassionate and humble.
Do not repay evil with evil or insult
with insult. On the contrary, repay evil
with blessing, because to this you were
called so that you may inherit a blessing.*
1 PETER 3:8–9 NIV

UNDERSTAND

- Why do you think our revenge reflex is
  often stronger than our compassion reflex?
- When have you been successful in
  repaying an insult with grace?

APPLY

Aside from a big bag of Halloween candy, there
are few things that seem as sweet and enticing as revenge. But both diving head-first into
a candy stash and paying someone back for
the wrong they did can leave us feeling sick.

The sugar overload leads to a belly ache, and revenge will lead to heartache.

Still, the world continues to tell us that we must stick up for ourselves. *Don't be a weakling! Put on your big-girl pants and get payback!* However, this attitude actually leaves us as slaves of our own desires and gratification. But God's way is the strongest way.

Love. Compassion. Humility. Repay evil with good. These are the very characteristics of Jesus Christ our Savior. If you want to be truly strong in the power of Jesus, follow His example in these things, and you'll receive blessings in this life and in eternity.

PRAY

Jesus, Peter is challenging me to take on some of Your very best characteristics in these verses. They sound so unlike me though. I know I can't be this person without Your help. Transform me from the inside out, Jesus. I am called to have sympathy, love, compassion, and humility. Lead me in all of these things, Savior. Amen.

Let Him In

Read Revelation 3:14–22

KEY VERSE

Here I am! I stand at the door and knock. If anyone hears my voice and opens the door, I will come in and eat with that person, and they with me.
REVELATION 3:20 NIV

UNDERSTAND

- In what ways do you hear Christ's knock?
- Is it enough to hear His voice?
- What is the significance of opening the door? Of eating together?

APPLY

We serve a Savior who comes to us as a friend. Who seeks us out. Who knocks on the door of our heart, calls out, "I'm here!" and delights in the moment we open the door to enter into fellowship with Him.

His knocking on the door may seem like an insignificant thing, but think of it this way: Jesus Christ is the King of kings and Lord of lords.

He is the Son of God and the Redeemer of the entire human race. Just one of these roles alone should make it impossible for us to have access to Him, let alone having Him come to us. But the fact remains that He cares for each of us so much and longs to spend time with us, so He comes. He stands at the door, knocks, and calls out, "I'm here!"

Today, prepare a feast of fellowship with Jesus. Lay a table of praise, and invite Him in. Listen to His voice and His ever-steadfast heart for You. And live in His love.

PRAY

Father, I'm listening intently for Your knock. When I hear Your voice, I will throw wide the door to my heart to invite You in. Come, eat with me. Let's talk and laugh and cry together. It is my heart's longing to know You more and more. Amen.

Simplicity and Sincerity

Read 2 Corinthians 1:12–24

KEY VERSE

For our boast is this, the testimony of our conscience, that we behaved in the world with simplicity and godly sincerity, not by earthly wisdom but by the grace of God, and supremely so toward you.

2 CORINTHIANS 1:12 ESV

UNDERSTAND

- Why do you think Paul is urging Christians to live with "simplicity and godly sincerity"?
- What pitfalls can come with living by "earthly wisdom"?
- In what ways can you simplify and live a more sincere life?

APPLY

It can be exhausting to try to keep up with current popular thought. From health and nutrition studies to politics and science, everything, it seems, is in a constant state of flux. It's impossible to know what the world sees as right and wrong, what's up and down, what's left and right.

While we should be aware of what's going on around us (we do live as nomads on earth, after all), Paul urges us not to get caught up in "earthly wisdom" but rather live simply and with godly sincerity. What does this look like? When we follow Christ's commands—love God and love others—we are shining the light of the Father in a dark and confusing place. And reflecting a sincere heart in everything we do shows the world that we are focused and grounded in a life-giving faith. Living such a life will attract others to the saving grace of Christ!

PRAY

Jesus, I've tried for too long to live the way the world tells me I should. It's exhausting trying to have it all, understand it all, do it all, and look flawless in the process. Give me Your wisdom to know what is essential: love, generosity, truth, forgiveness. Help me to live a life of simplicity and sincerity rooted in You. Amen.

Good Medicine

∽

Read Proverbs 17:13–28

KEY VERSE

A joyful heart is good medicine,
but a crushed spirit dries up the bones.
PROVERBS 17:22 ESV

UNDERSTAND

- Who or what can make you laugh no matter what?
- Who can you be joyously silly with?
- What situation or friend needs an infusion of joy today?

APPLY

The writer of Proverbs tucked this little verse in the middle of a string of warnings—hard issues that life throws our way as well as pitfalls and types of people to avoid. From fights and foolish financial decisions to corruption and lying, it's a laundry list of pathways to ruin.

But, the writer seems to say, joy in the middle of all of these things is good medicine—just what the doctor ordered.

Life is hard. Every day brings troubles—Jesus tells us so in Matthew 6:34—but how we choose to view and deal with those troubles is up to us. Look hard enough, and joy can be found in any situation. And viewed at the right angle and with a joyful heart, you may even find bright pockets of laughter in the darkest places.

Do you need an infusion of joy today? Look for the unique ways that God is shining light into your everyday life. And share that joy with others!

PRAY

Joyful Father, I am so thankful that You are a God who delights in laughter. You invite me to unburden my spirit (Psalm 55:22), and joy comes rushing in. Show me how to cultivate a heart bursting with Your hope and joy so I can share it with others. Give me pockets of laughter throughout my day. May it be Your soothing cure to my parched spirit and be a good medicine for everyone around me. Amen.

1/1

No Distractions

∽

Read Proverbs 4:18–27

KEY VERSES

Look straight ahead, and fix your eyes on what lies before you. Mark out a straight path for your feet; stay on the safe path. Don't get sidetracked; keep your feet from following evil.
PROVERBS 4:25–27 NLT

UNDERSTAND

- What distractions threaten to lead you off God's safe path? *what others want for selfish gain*
- What or whom are you fixing your eyes on as you walk through life? *Lord and Salvation the forever lasting ental life*
- What are some of the consequences of getting sidetracked from God's safe path? *Soek in hell Not showing our self.*

Bring outhos closer to Cpd BE are found no matter what

APPLY

Driver's-ed instructors and parents of permit-holding teens have the tough job of teaching young drivers the importance of avoiding distractions. Even before the days of digital devices and vehicles with touch screens, sound systems, radios, other passengers, and the goings-on outside a car could easily tempt gazes from looking straight ahead, focused on the pavement between the lines of the highway.

Life has even more dangerous distractions—some that Satan sets as enticing temptations that can lead us straight to disaster when we avert our eyes from God's path and our feet follow our gaze.

Look straight ahead, daughter of God. Your Brother, Jesus, stands before you on the straight path. Look farther, cherished one. Your Father laid the length of your journey before you. Look inside you, loved girl. Your Helper, the Holy Spirit, will make each of your steps forward confident.

Pray

Father, I admit that I am prone to wander, prone to distractions, prone to getting sidetracked. Forgive me when my eyes veer from You. Shine Your light on the safe path and nudge me back onto the straight way when necessary. I am following You and only You with my whole heart, soul, mind, and strength. Thank You for being a perfect leader. Amen.

You Are Powerful

❧

Read Romans 8:9–17

KEY VERSE

*The Spirit of God, who raised
Jesus from the dead, lives in you.*
ROMANS 8:11 NLT

UNDERSTAND

- When have you felt the Holy Spirit's power
  in your life? *@ J and their for after*
- Is there anything the Holy Spirit can't do? *No*
- What might you be doing (even unintentionally) to hinder the Holy Spirit's power in
  your life? *Show the good deeds
  he's done within my life spreading
  his word* APPLY

We serve an amazing God. The Creator of the
universe holds sway over all. He is almighty,
all-knowing, majestic in wonder, and powerful
beyond all comprehension. He holds all time,
matter, space, and dimension in His hand, and
as the Father, He cares for each of His children
with an overwhelming love.

The third Person of the Trinity—the Holy

Spirit—shares all these same attributes as the Father. And that Spirit lives in the heart of every believer, giving us access to God's power. The same power that brought Jesus *back to life* lives inside you!

Are you fearful of what life may throw at you? Sister, *you have God's power inside you*! Are you anxious, worried about today and to-morrow? You are an heir to God's glory. Are you afraid of messing up again? Listen to the voice of the Spirit, and you'll find the guidance you need.

PRAY

Spirit of God, move mightily in me. I am humbled and honored when I realize it was Your power that brought Jesus back to life. It was Your power that conquered death once and for all. And it is Your power that makes my salvation possible. All of that is enough, but You are my Helper and Guide. I ask You this morning to make me bold, fearless, confident, and powerful in the name of Jesus Christ to do big things for the Father's glory. Amen.

Challenge Yourself

Read Philippians 3:7–21

KEY VERSES

I do not say that I have received this or have already become perfect. But I keep going on to make that life my own as Christ Jesus made me His own. . . . My eyes are on the crown. I want to win the race and get the crown of God's call from heaven through Christ Jesus.
PHILIPPIANS 3:12, 14 NLV

UNDERSTAND

- What are you willing to sacrifice in order to become more like Jesus Christ?
- How can you push yourself in your faith to complete the race where the finish line is heaven?

APPLY

If anyone should've been satisfied with the state of his faith, it was the apostle Paul. This giant of the early Church experienced a miraculous conversion (see Acts 9), after which he became a world missionary. He wrote nearly half of the

New Testament and endured persecution and prosecution for the sake of sharing Jesus Christ. And yet, he knew he still had more growth to do, pressing himself closer to Jesus.

When you accepted Jesus into your life, it wasn't the end of the journey. Whether we've been a Christian for decades or are new to faith, each of us has space to advance toward our ultimate goal of eternal life with the Father, Son, and Holy Spirit in heaven.

What are you doing today to run the race? Sprinting, jogging, or walking, we're each at our own pace. Keep going and do not give up!

PRAY

God, I am ready for this challenge. This is a race that fills me with joy, and I want to run with excellence. Pick me up when I stumble, and set me on solid footing so I will run again. Amen.

What We Can Understand

❦

Read 1 Corinthians 13

KEY VERSES

When I was a child, I spoke and thought and reasoned as a child. But when I grew up, I put away childish things. Now we see things imperfectly, like puzzling reflections in a mirror, but then we will see everything with perfect clarity. All that I know now is partial and incomplete, but then I will know everything completely, just as God now knows me completely.

1 CORINTHIANS 13:11–12 NLT

UNDERSTAND

- How has your faith grown and changed since you became a Christian? In the past five years? In the past decade?
- What is something that you understand about God now that you didn't understand earlier in your faith journey?

APPLY

Because God made humans in His image, one of the amazing things about us is that we can learn and grow and transform over time. As our bodies grow from infancy, our minds are able to grasp more complex and abstract ideas, and personal experience can help us understand others and become more sympathetic with what they're going through.

But even in all these things, there are still many mysteries about God and about our faith that we cannot understand this side of heaven. Paul describes seeing these things as reflections in a mirror, which are backward and distorted. Today, you can take heart knowing that God gives us the understanding we need to grow on earth and the promise of full understanding when we are with Him in heaven someday.

Pray

Father, thank You for the ability to learn, grow, and mature in my understanding and in my faith in You. Even though I can't understand everything this side of heaven, I want to keep gaining new insight into Your heart, Your desires, and Your plan for me. Amen.

He Picks You Up

Read Psalm 40

KEY VERSE

He lifted me out of the pit of despair, out of the mud and the mire. He set my feet on solid ground and steadied me as I walked along.
PSALM 40:2 NLT

UNDERSTAND

- How has God lifted you up in the past?
- Has God ever used another person to pick you up, set you on solid ground, and steady you as you walked along? How did you realize God was using that person?

APPLY

Nobody—not even the most self-sufficient among us—can go through life alone. We each have our own struggles, temptations, pitfalls, and burdens that weigh us down and threaten to pull us into what Psalm 40:2 calls a "pit of despair."

Because our Savior, Jesus Christ, stepped out of heaven and lived on earth, He experienced all these same issues. And He is faithful to lift us up out of any muddy pit of sin and shame we may find ourselves in.

There are any number of ways He rescues us. From the encouragement and intervention of a friend or a new sense of hope given to us by the Holy Spirit to a new perspective on a problem or a new purpose and peace that passes understanding—in a matter of a moment, the Father God can set you on solid ground.

If you're in a pit—no matter how deep it is—cry out to God. No hole is your ultimate destination. He will hear you and is faithful to answer. Soon you'll find yourself safely in His arms.

PRAY

God, thank You for rescuing me. For pulling me out, cleaning me up, and giving me the confidence to walk ahead. Stay with me, and keep me from stumbling or jumping head-first into another pit of my own making. Amen.

God Is in Your Corner

Read Hebrews 13:6–19

KEY VERSE

So we say with confidence, "The Lord is my helper; I will not be afraid. What can mere mortals do to me?"

HEBREWS 13:6 NIV

UNDERSTAND

- Can trust in God and fear exist at the same time? Why or why not?
- When anxiety starts to creep in, what can you do to remember that God is on your side?

APPLY

Confidence is such an attractive quality, isn't it? Whether it's someone who can easily command the attention of the room or speaks in public flawlessly or simply excels at their job, it's inspiring and motivating to see someone who has it all figured out. Spoiler alert: the truth is that most of the time, even confident people have real fears.

Real, lasting confidence isn't something that comes from within us and our abilities. And confidence that truly conquers fear is rooted in the fact that, as Christians, we have God on our side. He is fighting for us, protecting us, and making us strong in spirit, heart, and mind.

Where in your life do you need an extra dose of confidence? The Lord is your Helper. All you need to do is ask for His guidance and His help. With Him in your corner, you can overcome anything!

PRAY

Father, I need Your help. I trust You, but fear keeps trying to force its way into my heart and mind. I can't shake these feelings of uncertainty. My brain keeps fretting over scenarios that I know will probably never happen, but I can't stop the thoughts by myself. Fill me with Your peace. Give me the confidence that You are in control and You want the best for me. Amen.

You Cannot Lose God's Love

∽

Read Psalm 136

KEY VERSE

Give thanks to the God of heaven.
His love endures forever.
PSALM 136:26 NIV

UNDERSTAND

- How does the fact that you cannot lose God's love affect your relationship with Him?
- Are you ever guarded in what you say to Him? Why or why not?
- How is God's love better than any other love?

APPLY

Psalm 136 repeats the phrase "His love endures forever" twenty-six times. It's as if the writer knows how easily we forget God's faithfulness, so after each statement, he reminds us (and himself), "His love endures forever."

The fact remains, if we are children of the God of heaven, we cannot lose His love. We are His forever—chosen, bought at a price, accepted, forgiven, redeemed, and a full heir to His kingdom.

Yet still we mess up, and doubt creeps in. We're not good enough. Not worthy of being forgiven for the same sin. . .again.

His love endures forever.

We worry and fret, anxious thoughts overtake us as we stumble through life. Forgetting that we've been saved and are protected by a mighty God, we try to fight our battles ourselves, sometimes pushing Him away.

His love endures forever.

You cannot lose His love, friend. Rest in that promise, and thank Him for His steadfastness today.

PRAY

Unending God, I see Your care for me everywhere. From the beauty of Your creation and the blessings You so generously lavish on me to the people You have placed in my life and the unique talents You have made in me, I feel Your love with every breath I take. Thank You for choosing me. Thank You for loving me always and forever. Amen.

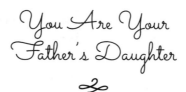

You Are Your Father's Daughter

Read 1 John 3:1-10

KEY VERSE

See how very much our Father loves us, for he calls us his children, and that is what we are!

1 JOHN 3:1 NLT

UNDERSTAND

- When you are getting to know someone, how do you explain and define yourself to them?
- In what ways do you struggle with your identity?
- How has your identity changed throughout your lifetime?

APPLY

Who are you? Mom, grandmother, daughter, granddaughter, niece, aunt, wife? Do you identify yourself as your occupation or a hobby or volunteer work or ministry?

All these things are good, and they do play a part in the way we interact with others, but not one of these labels is lasting. Relationships, jobs, hobbies, volunteer opportunities, and even some ministries are part of our lives only for a season. In reality, our identity has nothing to do with what we *do*. Instead, our identity is grounded in the fact that we are handpicked daughters of God the Father. We are sisters to our risen Savior and King, Jesus Christ, and forever counted as forgiven, saved, and standing in the grace of God.

So, when life is in upheaval, when you're not sure who you are, instead remember *whose* you are.

PRAY

When my life, my roles, and my relationships are in flux, Father, remind me who I am. I am Yours. I am a daughter of the King. I am claimed by Jesus as a sister. I am a vital part of the Body of Christ. I am forgiven, cherished, loved, and encouraged in You. Your identity is what I need. When people see me, let me fade into the background, and may Your light shine! Amen.

Your Circumstance Does Not Define You

Read 2 Corinthians 13:3-10

KEY VERSE

For to be sure, he was crucified in weakness, yet he lives by God's power. Likewise, we are weak in him, yet by God's power we will live with him in our dealing with you.

2 CORINTHIANS 13:4 NIV

UNDERSTAND

- Has weakness or struggle ever resulted in positive results for you? How?
- How does acknowledging your own weakness make room for God's power in your life?

APPLY

Sometimes we forget that Jesus struggled while He lived on earth. He understood the Father's plan for Him to die for the sins of the world. Jesus was fully committed to the plan, but in the hours before His arrest, trial, and execution, He

asked His Father to consider another way
(see Luke 22:42).

Jesus died at the hands of humankind—
painfully, pitifully, and shamefully. Yet it isn't
the weakness of Jesus' death that defines Him.
It's the power of God's victorious strength that
brought Him back to life that defines Jesus
Christ.

It's the same for God's children. We each
struggle in our own way. We live in a world filled
with evil, and each of us has times of weakness,
frustration, desperation, and shame; yet not
even the direst of circumstance defines us. We
are defined by God's victorious strength working in us and through us.

PRAY

*Almighty God, sometimes life feels like an
unending struggle. I know my own efforts are
futile, and I know these challenges aren't me—
they're just things that are happening to me.
Today I'm asking You to step in with Your
power. Cover me, Father, and I know You
will take care of it all. Amen.*

Rely on Him

⸺

Read Psalm 33:16–22

KEY VERSES

Don't count on your warhorse to give you victory—for all its strength, it cannot save you. But the LORD watches over those who fear him, those who rely on his unfailing love.

PSALM 33:17–18 NLT

UNDERSTAND

- Have you ever put your faith in someone or something that left you disappointed? What did you learn from that experience?
- How do you know you can trust God to take care of you?

APPLY

Scripture uses the beautiful Shepherd/sheep analogy to describe our relationship with God. Passages like Psalm 23 can fill us with peace and security to know that He takes care of us no matter what.

But just like sheep, we sometimes make dumb choices about who or what to trust. Ever been burned by the latest self-help craze? Has a friend or family member let you down? Maybe someone betrayed a trust after you shared something deeply personal. Quick fixes and three steps to a brand-new you can leave us feeling defeated, empty, and hopeless.

But our Great Shepherd is there, always seeking us, calling us back to Him. His love is unfailing, and His saving grace is absolute. Trust in Him to guide you, to protect you, to make your path clear for safe passage to eternity with Him.

PRAY

Thank You for watching over me, Father. You keep me safe and preserve my life in ways that I won't know this side of heaven. Your strength is what I put my trust in—not my own, not other people's. I am imperfect, and others will let me down whether they mean to or not. Your redeeming love lifts me up and holds me steady even in hard times. Amen.

Sing, Sing a Song

Read Psalm 149

KEY VERSE

*Praise the LORD! Sing to the LORD
a new song. Sing his praises in
the assembly of the faithful.*

PSALM 149:1 NLT

UNDERSTAND

Singing your song

What is your favorite way to make a
joyful noise to the Lord? Favorite song?

- How does actually singing praises to the
  Lord differ from having a song in your heart
  or simply thinking about His goodness?

- What does God's gift of music mean
  to you? *It allows for enornall*
  Block others out that leads me from
  whats ment for me

APPLY

What song does your heart sing this morning?
Whether you're humming an ancient hymn, a
popular worship song, or your original melody
of praise, God hears them all and accepts heart-
felt musical worship with delight.

Maybe your heart is silent today. Perhaps

singing is the last thing you can do when you're going through a difficult season. God sees you struggle, He is with you, and He understands.

Today, whether you're already singing or still silent, ask the Lord to renew you and give you a new song. Find pockets of praise and joy in living for Him, and take hold of the power of praise. Singing of His love and might will fortify you for the next thing life throws your way. Cultivating a habit of song is a beautiful way to praise God alone and with others. Today and every day sing, sing a song!

Pray

God, I will sing praises to You when I awake and when I lie down at night—and every moment between. Give me a song in my heart and a melody on my lips to honor You with every note. Thank You for the gift of music and how it can touch my heart in such a powerful way. I am overwhelmed by Your goodness! Amen.

He Is Near to the Brokenhearted

❧

Read Psalm 34

KEY VERSES

The LORD is near to the brokenhearted and saves the crushed in spirit. Many are the afflictions of the righteous, but the LORD delivers him out of them all.

PSALM 34:18–19 ESV

UNDERSTAND

- Do you feel the presence of God more during times of joy or times of sorrow? Why? *Both*

- Think about a time when you called out to God with a crushed spirit. How did He respond? *put things and People in front.*

APPLY

God's Word doesn't promise a life of unbridled bliss for God's children. On the contrary, Jesus tells us in John 16:33 (NLT), "Here on earth you will have many trials and sorrows."

But God is near, and during life's toughest

situations, He will rescue us from despair. His path will guide us through and give us the strength to overcome anything. Maybe you've seen friends or family go through impossible things like this and come out the other side stronger in their faith.

Yes, God will walk with us, carrying us when necessary, through life's many trials and sorrows. But the best news of all is what Jesus said in John 16, right after telling us to expect difficult times. "But take heart," He says in the second half of verse 33, "because I have overcome the world." Christ wins. We are victorious in Him.

PRAY

Lord of all my days, thank You for always being near. I love to celebrate with You when things are going well, but I am also deeply grateful that You come even closer when I am brokenhearted, grieving, and crushed in spirit. You are faithful to bring me through and are so patient with me when I am struggling. I don't deserve such kindness, but I am so thankful for it! Amen.

You Can Live without Fear

❧

Read Isaiah 41:8-14

KEY VERSES

*"For I have chosen you and will not throw
you away. Don't be afraid, for I am with you.
Don't be discouraged, for I am your God.
I will strengthen you and help you. I will hold
you up with my victorious right hand."*

ISAIAH 41:9-10 NLT

UNDERSTAND

- Have you ever considered the fact that God will not throw you away? How does that fact make you feel? Strong
- How can knowing God is with you make you less fearful? Less discouraged?

APPLY

Fear is something like a strain of influenza. Just when we think we've figured out the proper vaccine to safeguard ourselves, the virus changes, and the flu rears its ugly head once again. And just when we think we've overcome our fear, some new worry or anxiety pops up, and anxious thoughts return, sometimes leaving us down for the count.

The only true cure for fear is unconditional trust in God. Faith that He will keep His promises all throughout scripture. He has chosen you. He will not throw you away. He is with you. He is your God who will strengthen you and help you. He will hold you up.

Do you believe Him? When your fears threaten to take over again, remember His faithfulness in keeping these promises in the past. He has never failed you yet, and He will not fail you now.

PRAY

Almighty God, no matter what I face, I know You are with me. You chose me for a reason, and I know You have a perfect plan for me safe inside Your will. Be near me, Father, especially when I am feeling unsure of the way. Hold me up when I can't stand on my own, and usher me into Your victorious presence forevermore. Amen.

He Thinks of You

Read Matthew 10:24–31

KEY VERSES

"Are not two small birds sold for a very small piece of money? And yet not one of the birds falls to the earth without your Father knowing it. God knows how many hairs you have on your head. So do not be afraid. You are more important than many small birds."

MATTHEW 10:29–31 NLV

UNDERSTAND

- If you've ever been forgotten or over-looked, how can it change your perspective to know that God thinks about you?
- How does it make you feel that God knows you so well that He has the hairs on your head numbered?

APPLY

Our God is not some far-off, cosmic force who created us and then sat back to watch us implode. Even in the middle of our own self-implosion (sin), God is there, loving us back to

Himself so we can be in a right relationship with Him.

Maybe today you're feeling forgotten by friends or family. Rejected, overlooked, unloved. When other humans fail us, God is steadfast in His care. He celebrates with us in our victories and comforts us in our tragedies. He rejoices when we make good choices and lovingly disciplines us back to the right path in our failures. We are on His mind and constantly in His heart.

Today, relax in His constant care. Thank Him for knowing you and loving you so perfectly. You are priceless to Him.

PRAY

Father, sometimes I feel overlooked, unloved, and forgotten by others. I try not to dwell on it, but it hurts me deeply. Help me to remember that I am always in Your thoughts. You love me with a fierce love. When it comes down to it, God, You are all I need. Amen.

Get Out of Your Comfort Zone

Read 1 Peter 4:1–11

KEY VERSE

If anyone speaks, they should do so as one who speaks the very words of God. If anyone serves, they should do so with the strength God provides, so that in all things God may be praised through Jesus Christ. To him be the glory and the power for ever and ever.

1 PETER 4:11 NIV

UNDERSTAND

- Have you ever gone "all in" for God's kingdom work? Why or why not?
- How far out of your comfort zone are you willing to go for your Savior?

APPLY

Do you ever see an opportunity to do something for God's kingdom, but your own insecurities stop you short of action? Often, we talk ourselves out of good intentions that may have been sparked in our hearts by the Lord Himself.

In 1 Peter 4, the apostle Peter reminds us

that God has equipped us to step forth boldly to act in His name. When we're following our Father's lead, it's not about staying where we are comfortable. It's about trusting Him with everything—and that means stepping out in faith.

Peter literally stepped out of a boat in faith and walked on water in the middle of a storm. And when he took his eyes off Jesus and started to sink, Jesus lifted him again (see Matthew 14:22-33).

If Peter could walk on water, there is nothing you cannot do if Jesus calls you to it. Step out of your comfort zone today!

Pray

God, I know if I'm left to my own devices, I'll stay where I am, comfortable in my own little spot. Today I'm asking You to stretch me. Lead me boldly out of my comfort zone, and I will serve mightily for Your glory. Amen.

About the Author

Annie Tipton wrote her first story at the ripe old age of two when she asked her mom to write it down for her. (Hey, she was just two—she didn't know how to make letters yet!) Since then she has read and written many words as a student, newspaper reporter, author, and editor. Annie loves snow (which is a good thing because she lives in Ohio), wearing scarves, eating sushi, playing Scrabble, and spending time with friends and family.

A___ B+___ C_____ No thanks

Straight through

2-3 hundred for classes

10 pm or 10:30 pm

(4pm)